First World War
and Army of Occupation
War Diary
France, Belgium and Germany

34 DIVISION
Divisional Troops
Royal Army Service Corps
Divisional Train (229,230,231,232 Companies) (A.S.C.)
12 January 1915 - 31 July 1919

WO95/2454/4

Published by

The Naval & Military Press Ltd

Unit 10 Ridgewood Industrial Park,

Uckfield, East Sussex,

TN22 5QE England

Tel: +44 (0) 1825 749494

www.naval-military-press.com

www.nmarchive.com

This diary has been reprinted in facsimile from the original. Any imperfections are inevitably reproduced and the quality may fall short of modern type and cartographic standards.

© Crown Copyright
Images reproduced by permission of The National Archives, London, England, 2015.

Contents

Document type	Place/Title	Date From	Date To
Heading	WO95/2454/4		
Heading	34th Division Divl Troops 34th Divl Train A.S.C. 1915 Jan-1919 Jly		
War Diary	Aldershot	12/01/1915	03/02/1915
War Diary	Buxton	10/02/1915	06/03/1915
War Diary	Derby	30/04/1915	13/07/1915
War Diary	Kirkby Malzeard Camp.	19/07/1915	22/08/1915
War Diary	Windmill Hill Camp.	31/08/1915	23/09/1915
War Diary	Warminster	26/09/1915	25/12/1915
Heading	34th Div. Train Vol I Jan 16-Dec 18		
War Diary	Ebblinghem	09/01/1916	23/01/1916
War Diary	Blaringhem	24/01/1916	31/01/1916
War Diary	Reninghelst	01/01/1916	31/01/1916
Heading	34th Div Train Vol 2		
War Diary	Blaringhe B23 A Sheet 36A	01/02/1916	01/02/1916
War Diary	B 23 A Sheet 36 A	01/02/1916	09/02/1916
War Diary	Blaringhem	11/02/1916	24/02/1916
War Diary	Croix Du Bac	25/02/1916	27/02/1916
Heading	34 Div Train Vol 3		
War Diary	Croix Du Bac	01/03/1916	14/04/1916
War Diary	Salperwick	17/04/1916	06/05/1916
War Diary	Behencourt	06/05/1916	30/06/1916
Miscellaneous	Allotment of Reserve Rations.	15/06/1916	15/06/1916
Miscellaneous	Headquarters G. 34th Division	03/08/1916	03/08/1916
War Diary	Dernancourt	01/07/1916	05/07/1916
War Diary	Behencourt	05/07/1916	07/07/1916
War Diary	Lavieville	08/07/1916	19/07/1916
War Diary	Behencourt	20/07/1916	29/07/1916
War Diary	W.20 D	30/07/1916	31/07/1916
Miscellaneous	Headquarters G. 34th Division	01/09/1916	01/09/1916
War Diary	W.20.d Albert Combined Sheet.	01/08/1916	14/08/1916
War Diary	Behencourt	15/08/1916	16/08/1916
War Diary	Cardonnette	17/08/1916	17/08/1916
War Diary	Hallencourt	18/08/1916	19/08/1916
War Diary	Doulieu	20/08/1916	24/08/1916
War Diary	Croix Du Bac	25/08/1916	27/08/1916
Miscellaneous	Headquarters G. 34th Division.	05/10/1916	05/10/1916
War Diary	Croix Du Bac	01/09/1916	30/09/1916
Miscellaneous	Headquarters "G" 34th Division	01/11/1916	01/11/1916
War Diary	Croix Du Bac	01/10/1916	31/10/1916
Miscellaneous	Headquarters 34th Division G	03/12/1916	03/12/1916
War Diary	Croix Du Bac	01/11/1916	29/11/1916
Miscellaneous	Headquarters 34th Division G.	12/01/1917	12/01/1917
War Diary	Croix Du Bac	01/12/1916	26/01/1917
War Diary	Fletre	27/01/1917	18/02/1917
War Diary	Rombly	19/02/1917	20/02/1917
War Diary	Frevillers	21/02/1917	21/02/1917
War Diary	Chelers	22/02/1917	28/02/1917
Miscellaneous	H.Q. 34th Division. G	05/04/1917	05/04/1917
War Diary	Chelers	01/03/1917	17/03/1917

Type	Location	From	To
War Diary	Camp.E.29.B.4.6	18/03/1917	25/03/1917
War Diary	Camp E. 2.1.B. 4.6	25/03/1917	29/03/1917
Miscellaneous	H.Q. 34th Division G	03/05/1917	03/05/1917
War Diary	Camp.E.29.B.4.6	02/04/1917	14/04/1917
War Diary	Chelers	15/04/1917	20/04/1917
War Diary	Laresset	21/04/1917	01/05/1917
War Diary	Le Cauroy	02/05/1917	06/05/1917
War Diary	Bernaville	07/05/1917	30/05/1917
War Diary	Camp (G.14. A. 51.B)	31/05/1917	17/06/1917
War Diary	Camp.G.14 A.	18/06/1917	27/06/1917
Miscellaneous	H.Q. 34th Division G.S.	08/08/1917	08/08/1917
War Diary	Hermaville	01/07/1917	06/07/1917
War Diary	Peronne	09/07/1917	10/07/1917
War Diary	Roisel	11/07/1917	31/07/1917
Miscellaneous	H.Q. 34th Division G.S.	08/09/1917	08/09/1917
War Diary	Roisel	01/08/1917	31/08/1917
Miscellaneous	H.Q. 34th Division G.S.	12/10/1917	12/10/1917
War Diary	Roisel	01/09/1917	29/09/1917
War Diary	Basseux	30/09/1917	30/09/1917
Miscellaneous	H.Q. 34th Division G.	07/11/1917	07/11/1917
War Diary	Basseux	02/10/1917	07/10/1917
War Diary	Proven	08/10/1917	14/10/1917
War Diary	A.24.G.88	18/10/1917	28/10/1917
War Diary	Achiet	29/10/1917	31/10/1917
Miscellaneous	H.Q. 34th Dis. G.	13/12/1917	13/12/1917
War Diary	Achiet-Le-Petit	01/11/1917	01/11/1917
War Diary	Boisleux-Au-Mont	02/11/1917	29/11/1917
Miscellaneous	H.Q. 34th Division G.	05/02/1918	05/02/1918
War Diary	Boisleux-Au-Mont	05/01/1918	27/01/1918
War Diary	Boiry-St-Rictrude	29/01/1918	10/02/1918
War Diary	Berlencourt	11/02/1918	28/02/1918
Miscellaneous	H.Q. 34th Division G.S.	20/04/1918	20/04/1918
War Diary	Boiry-St-Rictrude	01/03/1918	22/03/1918
War Diary	Douchy-Les-Ayette	23/03/1918	24/03/1918
War Diary	Basseux	25/03/1918	25/03/1918
War Diary	Le Cauroy	26/03/1918	26/03/1918
War Diary	Auxi-Le-Chateau	27/03/1918	27/03/1918
War Diary	Merville	28/03/1918	29/03/1918
War Diary	Le Sart	31/03/1918	31/03/1918
War Diary	Gommiecourt	22/03/1918	22/03/1918
War Diary	Ayette Adinfer	23/03/1918	23/03/1918
War Diary	Adinfer Basseux	24/03/1918	24/03/1918
War Diary	Basseux Le Cauroy	25/03/1918	25/03/1918
War Diary	Le Couroy Auxi-Le-Chatean	26/03/1918	26/03/1918
War Diary	Auxi-Le-Chatean	27/03/1918	27/03/1918
War Diary	Merville	28/03/1918	30/03/1918
War Diary	Merville Steenwerck	31/03/1918	31/03/1918
Miscellaneous	H.Q. 34th Division G.S.	15/05/1918	15/05/1918
War Diary	Steenwerck	01/04/1918	08/04/1918
War Diary	S Of B-S Road	09/04/1918	11/04/1918
War Diary	Le Grand Hazard	12/04/1918	12/04/1918
War Diary	Godwaerswelde	13/04/1918	17/04/1918
War Diary	Steenworde	18/04/1918	18/04/1918
War Diary	Geewerke	19/04/1918	22/04/1918
War Diary	St Janter	24/04/1918	24/04/1918
War Diary	Biezen	24/04/1918	29/04/1918

Type	Location	Start	End
War Diary	28.K.L.D.9.9	30/04/1918	30/04/1918
Miscellaneous	H.Q. 34th Division G.S.	22/06/1918	22/06/1918
War Diary	Camp. 28.K.L.D.9.9	01/05/1918	12/05/1918
War Diary	Rubrouk	13/05/1918	13/05/1918
War Diary	Nielles	16/05/1918	31/05/1918
Miscellaneous	H.Q. 34th Division G.	09/07/1918	09/07/1918
War Diary	Nielles	01/06/1918	04/06/1918
War Diary	Wierreeffroi	10/06/1918	11/06/1918
War Diary	Nielles	12/06/1918	17/06/1918
War Diary	Moulinet	18/06/1918	28/06/1918
War Diary	Elnes	29/06/1918	29/06/1918
War Diary	St. Momelin	30/06/1918	30/06/1918
Miscellaneous	H.Q. 34th Division G.S.	25/08/1918	25/08/1918
War Diary	Bambeque	01/07/1918	03/07/1918
War Diary	Couthove	04/07/1918	22/07/1918
War Diary	Forest Nr Longpont	27/07/1918	29/07/1918
Miscellaneous	H.Q. 34th Division G.S.	16/09/1918	16/09/1918
War Diary	Chouy	01/08/1918	03/08/1918
War Diary	Billy	04/08/1918	04/08/1918
War Diary	Mareuil	05/08/1918	05/08/1918
War Diary	Nanteuil	06/08/1918	06/08/1918
War Diary	Esquelbecq	07/08/1918	21/08/1918
War Diary	La Lovie	22/08/1918	29/08/1918
War Diary	K.21.b.9.4	30/08/1918	31/08/1918
Miscellaneous	H.Q. 34th Division G.S.	25/10/1918	25/10/1918
War Diary	K.21.b.9.4	01/09/1918	01/09/1918
War Diary	L.28.G.3.4	02/09/1918	17/09/1918
War Diary	27/R.5.C.1.7	18/09/1918	30/09/1918
Miscellaneous	By Registered Post.	27/12/1918	27/12/1918
War Diary	28/M.6	01/10/1918	01/10/1918
War Diary	Houthem-Hollebeke	02/10/1918	03/10/1918
War Diary	28.H.36	05/10/1918	05/10/1918
War Diary	28.H.30.D.	06/10/1918	17/10/1918
War Diary	J.32.C.	18/10/1918	18/10/1918
War Diary	Gheluve	19/10/1918	19/10/1918
War Diary	28/Q.4.b.3.1	20/10/1918	21/10/1918
War Diary	28/R.14.C.2	22/10/1918	22/10/1918
War Diary	Lauwe	23/10/1918	29/10/1918
War Diary	29/H.11.G.2.9	30/10/1918	03/11/1918
War Diary	28/4.23.a.9.4	06/11/1918	15/11/1918
War Diary	Wattripont	16/11/1918	18/11/1918
War Diary	Lessines	21/11/1918	28/11/1918
Miscellaneous	Per Registered Post, D.A.G., 3rd Echelon.	02/02/1919	02/02/1919
War Diary	Lessines	05/12/1918	12/12/1918
War Diary	Soignies	14/12/1918	16/12/1918
War Diary	Courcelles	17/12/1918	18/12/1918
War Diary	Chatelet	19/12/1918	19/12/1918
War Diary	Profondeville	20/12/1918	24/01/1919
War Diary	Siegburg	25/01/1919	31/07/1919

waist/2+5+4 (a)

2015/2+5+4 (a)

34TH DIVISION
DIVL TROOPS

34TH DIVL TRAIN A.S.C.

1915 JAN — 1919 JLY

229-233 Cys
ASC

Army Form C. 2118

WAR DIARY
or
INTELLIGENCE SUMMARY of 34th Divisional Train, Army Service Corps.

(Erase heading not required.)

1915

Place	Date	Hour	Summary of Events and Information	Remarks and references to Appendices
Aldershot.	12.1.15.		Train formed: personnel only assembled. Numbers 229, 230 231 232 Companies. Major A.H.Roberts in command.	
	21.1.15.		Major H.W.A.Collum took over command.	
	3.2.15.		Designation altered to 41st Divisional Train.	
Buxton.	10.2.15.		The Train moved to BUXTON and was billetted in the EMPIRE HOTEL. Messing money at 1/9d per man per day drawn. Daily training of men in foot-drill and Physical Drill carried out.	
	12.2.15.		Lt.Col. W.M.H.ARMSTRONG took over the command.	
	15.2.15.		12 Country Carts received from DEPTFORD.	
	5.3.15.		Major H.W.A.COLLUM took over command.	
	6.3.15.		12 Riding and 16 Heavy Draught Horses received. Instruction in Riding and Driving given continuously after this date.	
Derby.	30.4.15.		The Train moved to DERBY, and was accomodated in hired buildings and billets, viz:- 229 C.V. in the Assembly Rooms and Edward Street School, 230 Coy. in Sitwell Street School, 231 Coy. in London Road School, and 232 Coy. in Derwent Street and St.Mary's Gate School. Rations drawn and 5½d per man messing money.	
	1.5.15.		Major L.H.Lloyd took over the command.	
	12.5.15.		Designation altered to 34th Divisional Train.	
	14.6.15.		6 Bain, 6 Studebaker, and 4 tip-carts arrived.	
	27.6.15.		Major E.G.Evans took over the command.	

N.G. Evans Lt Col
COMMANDING
34th DIVISIONAL TRAIN,
ARMY SERVICE CORPS.

Army Form C. 2118

WAR DIARY
or
INTELLIGENCE SUMMARY — of 34th Divisional Train, Army Service Corps.

(Erase heading not required.)

Instructions regarding War Diaries and Intelligence Summaries are contained in F.S. Regs., Part II. and the Staff Manual respectively. Title Pages will be prepared in manuscript.

Place	Date	Hour	Summary of Events and Information	Remarks and references to Appendices
Derby.	3.7.15.		Field Bakery, Field Butchery, Rly. Supply Det., 160th & 162nd D.U.Supply, arrived in Derby.	
	12.7.15.		50 H.D.Horses received and picketted in hired Field.	
	13.7.15.		Infectious Influenza in this last draft of horses.	
Kirkby Malzeard Camp	19.7.15.		The Train moved to KIRKBY MALZEARD CAMP 7 miles N.W. of RIPON, Yorks. Two Railway Trains used. No.232 Company left at Derby vo look after the 50 H.D.Horses with Influenza.	
	21.9.15.		The 34th Field Bakery commenced baking bread for the troops at RIPON, taking alternate days with 31st Field Bakery. All wagons employed on Transport duty daily.	
	24.7.15.		50 D.P.Rifles per Company arrived.	
	27.7.15.		Canteen opened, Contractor:- G.Whitley & Sons, Horton Street. Halifax.	
	29.7.15.		Horses started arriving; 28 today.	
	31.7.15.		13 chargers, 4 cobs, 38 heavy draught horses arrived	

34th DIVISIONAL TRAIN,
ARMY SERVICE CORPS.

Army Form C. 2118

WAR DIARY
or
INTELLIGENCE SUMMARY

of 34th Divisional Train, Army Service Corps.

(Erase heading not required.)

Instructions regarding War Diaries and Intelligence Summaries are contained in F.S. Regs., Part II. and the Staff Manual respectively. Title Pages will be prepared in manuscript.

Place	Date	Hour	Summary of Events and Information	Remarks and references to Appendices
Kirkby Malzeard Camp.	2.8.15.		9 Riding horses and 120 H.D.Horses arrived.	
	4.8.15.		84 H.D.Horses arrived.	
	5.8.15.		34 H.D.Horses arrived.	
	6.8.15.		20 Riders arrived.	
	7.8.15.		Harness received by 229, 230, 231 Coy's. and fitted to horses daily as quickly as possible.	
	11.8.15.		Inspection by Major-General Sir.A.J.Murray K.C.B., L.C.M.G., C.V.O., D.S.O., Deputy Chief of the Imperial General Staff. Unsatisfactory; the Companies had not had time to properly fit or clean the harness since its receipt, and there had been very heavy rain every day for the past week.	
	13.8.15.		22 Riding horses arrived.	
	14.8.15.		Horses inspected by Assistant Director of Remounts. Train completed with Limbered Wagons.	
	22.8.15.		Advance Party left at 7.30 pm for WINDMILL HILL, SALISBURY PLAIN: strength, 6 officers and 64 other ranks; 54 wagons horses, 26 wagons, under Capt.Mayne. Transport sent to assist Units of Division in obtaining camp equipment etc. Field Bakery and Butchery left for WINDMILL HILL CAMP.	
Windmill Hill Camp.	31.8.15.		Main body left for WINDMILL HILL CAMP, also 160th, 161st, and 162nd D.U.Supply. 158th & 159th D.U.Supply left Newcastle on Tyne with 11th Suffolks for Salisbury Plain.	

[signature]
COMMANDING
34th DIVISIONAL TRAIN,
ARMY SERVICE CORPS.

Army Form C. 2118

WAR DIARY
or
INTELLIGENCE SUMMARY

of 34th Divisional Train, Army Service Corps.

(Erase heading not required.)

Instructions regarding War Diaries and Intelligence Summaries are contained in F.S. Regs., Part II. and the Staff Manual respectively. Title Pages will be prepared in manuscript.

Place	Date	Hour	Summary of Events and Information	Remarks and references to Appendices
Windmill Hill Camp	8.9.15		Feeding Division undertaken. Field Bakery turning out about 20,000 loaves daily. Drawing Supplies by bulk from Supply Depot, TIDWORTH, and making detail issues to Brigades and Divisional Troops from Dumping Places, being carried out daily.	
	10.9.15		Inspection by Lt.Gen.Sit.A.Paget, C. in C. Southern Command. Satisfactory. G.O.C., 34th Division stated improvement was marked.	
	16.9.15		31 H.D.Horses arrived.	
	17.9.15		3 H.D.Horses transferred to Train from 18th Northumberland Fusiliers.	
	23.9.15		14 H.D.Horses arrived.	
Warminster.	26.9.15		232 Cov. by march route to WARMINSTER, bivouacing en route, on PARSONAGE DOWN.	
	27.9.15		230 " " "	
	28.9.15		231 " " "	
	30.9.15		Headquarters of Train moved to WARMINSTER by Rail.	

[signature] COMMANDING
34th DIVISIONAL TRAIN,
ARMY SERVICE CORPS.

Army Form C. 2118

WAR DIARY
or
INTELLIGENCE SUMMARY of 34th Divisional Train, Army Service Corps.
(Erase heading not required.)

Instructions regarding War Diaries and Intelligence Summaries are contained in F.S. Regs., Part II. and the Staff Manual respectively. Title Pages will be prepared in manuscript.

Place	Date	Hour	Summary of Events and Information	Remarks and references to Appendices
Warminster.	1.10.15.		229 Coy. by March Route to WARMINSTER, bivouacing en route on PARSONAGE DOWN.	
	2.10.15.		2/Lt.Hall with 23 wagons moved by march route with 152nd, 176th Bdes. R.F.A. & Div.Amm.Col. to CORTON, carrying Rations and Forage for R.A., bivouacing at CORTON.	
	3.10.15.		2/Lt.Harrison with 26 wagons moved by march route with Hdqrs. R.A., 160th, 175th Bdes R.F.A. to CORTON, carrying forage and rations for R.A., bivouacing at CORTON.	
	9.10.15.		Drawing supplies by bulk from Supply Depot, WARMINSTER and CODFORD, and making detail issues to Bdes. and Divl.Troops from Dumping Places, is being carried out daily.	
	4.10.15.		231 & 232 Coy's. moved to No.6.Camp Sutton Veny. H.D.	
			Horse Strength now down to 404/and 70 Riders, owing to 53 having been sent to Station Vetinary Hospital, BULFORD, on various dates	
	14.10.15.		Inspection by Maj.Genl.Landon. Train inspected on parade and convoy. Unsatisfactory on account of men's clothing, Coy'g being unable to obtain new issues.	
	18.10.15.		Train commenced musketry unde the Bde Musketry Officers and fired 5 practices on the open range.	
	24.10.15.		15 Riders and 24 L.D. horses arrived for the Field Ambulances.	
	25.10.15.		2/Lts. MacDonald and W.J.Deasley joined the Train for duty.	
	30.10.15.		24 H.D. horses received. 16 Riders taken over from Artillery.	

[signature]
COMMANDING
34th DIVISIONAL TRAIN,
ARMY SERVICE CORPS.

Army Form C. 2118.

WAR DIARY
or
INTELLIGENCE SUMMARY of 34th Divisional Train, Army Service Corps.

(*Erase heading not required.*)

Instructions regarding War Diaries and Intelligence Summaries are contained in F. S. Regs., Part II. and the Staff Manual respectively. Title pages will be prepared in manuscript.

Place	Date	Hour	Summary of Events and Information	Remarks and references to Appendices
Warminster	1.11.15.		28 H.D. horses received.	
	3.11.15.		70 H.D. transferred to 9th Prov. Bde., Canterbury, 60 H.D. to 6th Prov. Bde., 20 H.D. to 5th Prov. Bde., 10 H.D. to 140th H.B.	
	4.11.15.		Lieuts. Smeed and 2/Lts. Cameron and Wade transferred to 11th Divl. Train. 14 H.D. horses received.	
	8.11.15.		26 H.D. transferred to 38th Divl.Train, A.S.C., 48 H.D. to 39th Divl.Train.	
	9.11.15.		Field Ambulances arrive and are affiliated as follows: 104th F.A. to 230 Coy., 102nd F.A. to 231 Coy., 103rd F.A. to 232 Coy.	
	19.11.15.		Brig.Genl.Coke inspected Remounts.	

[signature]
COMMANDING
34th DIVISIONAL TRAIN,
ARMY SERVICE CORPS.

Army Form C. 2118.

WAR DIARY
or
INTELLIGENCE SUMMARY.

of 34th Divisional Train, Army Service Corps.

(Erase heading not required.)

Instructions regarding War Diaries and Intelligence Summaries are contained in F.S. Regs., Part II. and the Staff Manual respectively. Title pages will be prepared in manuscript.

Place	Date	Hour	Summary of Events and Information	Remarks and references to Appendices
Warminster	9.12.15		143 Mules arrive from Taunton. 28 H.D. horses transferred from Train.	
	10.12.15		37 Drivers received from Bradford Depot. 11th Divl. Train – only 11 fit.	
	13.12.15		Lord Derby's Recruits begin to arrive.	
	14.12.15		205 Mules arrive.	
	16.12.15		100 H.D. Horses transferred from Train. 30 Drivers received from Bradford Depot.	
	18.12.15		300 Mules arrive. 210 Trained Transport Drivers arrive from Park Royal.	
	19.12.15		193 H.D. transferred from Train. Total number of Mules in Train 648. Field Ambulances complete in personnel. 75 Recruits received to date.	
	20.12.15		Strength of Train in men and animals:— 717 all ranks, 648 Mules, 22 Unfit H.D. Horses, 29 L.D.	
	25.12.15		Orders received to reorganise Train on Horse basis.	

_____ COMMANDING
84th DIVISIONAL TRAIN,
ARMY SERVICE CORPS.

34 2 Srit- Prain
—————
rot: I

Jan '16
Dec '16

Army Form C. 2118.

WAR DIARY
or
INTELLIGENCE SUMMARY.

34th Div. Train A.S.C.

(Erase heading not required.)

Instructions regarding War Diaries and Intelligence Summaries are contained in F. S. Regs., Part II. and the Staff Manual respectively. Title pages will be prepared in manuscript.

Place	Date	Hour	Summary of Events and Information	Remarks and references to Appendices
Ebblinghem	9-1-16		Hdqrs. 34th Div. Tr. arrived here from England; billeted at EBBLINGHEM.	
	11-1-16		No. 2 Coy arrived here from England; billeted at LA CROSSE.	
	12-1-16		No. 3 Coy arrived here from England; billeted at CAMPAGNE.	
	13-1-16		No. 4 Coy arrived here from England; billeted at ESQUERDES.	
	15-1-16		Railhead ST. OMER. Brigade Refilling Points in Brigade areas.	
	19-1-16		Div. Refilling Point on the Road running North West from just where the D in CAMPAGNE (except R.A. whose full at BIENTQUES. HARREQUES through the N in CAMPAGNE.)	
	20-1-16		Div. Refilling Point on the AIRE-ARQUES road between the X roads at BELLE CROIX and the N in HARDREQUES.	
	23-1-16		The Division has D.A.C. & Div. Cavalry, Cyclist Coy, 209th Field Coy R.E., 102nd Fd. Ambulance (less 1 section) 103rd Fd. Ambulance, moved to BLARINGHEM, about 3 miles South of EBBLINGHEM.	
			D.A.C., Div. Cavalry & Cyclist Coy. proceeded into the "Forward area", attached to 8th Div. Lorries carried supplies for the 34th for those Units. Trains Supply wagons being used for Blankets. Attached to 9th Divn. for supplies from 25th. 209th Coy R.E., 102nd Fd. Amb. (less 1 section) 103rd Fd. Amb. drawing for themselves & 23rd/24th as follows: 209th Coy R.E. GRAND SEC BOIS, 102nd Fd Amb. (less 1 sec)	

2353 Wt. W2514/1454 700,000 5/15 D.D.&L. 209th Coy R.E., 102nd Fd. Amb. A.D.S.S./Forms/C. 2118.

Army Form C. 2118.

2

WAR DIARY
or
INTELLIGENCE SUMMARY.
(Erase heading not required.)

Instructions regarding War Diaries and Intelligence Summaries are contained in F. S. Regs., Part II. and the Staff Manual respectively. Title pages will be prepared in manuscript.

Place	Date	Hour	Summary of Events and Information	Remarks and references to Appendices
BLARINGHEM	24.1.16		and 103rd Fd.Amb'ce, PETIT SEC BOIS. Supply wagons of Train for 209th Bg R.E. 102nd Fd.Amb. (less 1 sect.) & 703rd Field Amb. proceeded loaded in 23rd Lorries carrying supplies for the 25th.	
	25.1.16		Railhead at STEENBECQUE. Refilling Point at WITTES for R.A. and 103rd Bde. Remainder at STEENBECQUE. 10.10 BAC (less 2 Bns) & 209th Fd.Coy R.E. proceeded into the "forward area" were attached to 23rd Div. Lieut Thompson & 2 personnel of No. 2 Coy of Train proceeded with the supply wagons, were attached to 23rd Div Train. 2/Lt Aitken proceeded as Supply Officer.	
	26.1.16		102nd Bde. (less 2 Bns) & 209th Fd. Coy by R.E. proceeded to YONNES Area where attached to 8th Div. Lieut Mitchell & 2 NCOs of No. 4 Coy of this Train accompanied supply wagons were attached to 8th Div. Train. 103rd Bde. refilling transferred to STEENBECQUE. Dumping direct from the Train & refilling in station yards STEENBECQUE for all except R.A. Fd.Amb's. Divnl. group. commenced.	
	31.1.16		10th Lincolns & 7th Suffolks (both of 102nd Bde) proceeded into forward area, joining from Lery will be attached to 23rd Divn, with supply & baggage wagons	

31.1.16

References:
HAZEBROUCK 5A.

Army Form C. 2118

WAR DIARY
or
INTELLIGENCE SUMMARY

(Erase heading not required.)

C.R.E. 17th Division

January

Place	Date	Hour	Summary of Events and Information	Remarks and references to Appendices
Renninghelst	1.1.16		Preparing orders for movement to Rest Area.	
	2.1.16		Advance party sent on to REST AREA. C.R.E. with YPRES and company A.D.M.S.	
	3.1.16		C.R.E. left to join 14th Corps. R.E. adjutant and 15th Division came up to take over.	
	3.1.16		Bivouacked party: field companies left for rest area by bus & train	
	4.1.16		Bivouacked parties of 2nd 15 Division companies taking over from us for fire.	
	5.1.16		Mantel position field companies field companies moved to rest area (half day halts)	
	6.1.16		Mantel position of holidays billets — Headquarters R.E. move to RESTANGE. 75th Company	
	7.1.16		Mantel position complete much and go to BLUE 77th Company at THAES. 78th Company at NORRECOURT 93rd Company at MONS COVE (HAZEBROUCK 5A mtps)	
	8.1.16 to 28/1/16		} In rest area — Companies refitting - drilling - musketry and pontooning.	
	29/1/16		Colonel Carpets joins as C.R.E.	
	29/1/16 to 31/1/16		} musketry — drill - marches and pontoons.	

for Heads Cap R.E.
for CRE 17 Division

84 Dis
Spain
Vol. 2

Army Form C. 2118

2

WAR DIARY
or
INTELLIGENCE SUMMARY
(Erase heading not required.)

34th Divl Train ASC

Instructions regarding War Diaries and Intelligence Summaries are contained in F.S. Regs., Part II. and the Staff Manual respectively. Title Pages will be prepared in manuscript.

Place	Date	Hour	Summary of Events and Information	Remarks and references to Appendices
BLARINGHE B23A Sheet 36A	1/2/16		22nd & 23rd Bn Northumberland Fusiliers proceded onto "Forward Area" taking their supply and baggage wagons	
	11/2/16		15th & 16th Royal Scots returned with baggage and supply wagons to 31st Divisional Area	
	5/2/16		10th Lincolns & 11th Suffolks proceeded to Forward Area with baggage and supply wagons. 69/104th Bde returned to 31st Divisional Area.	
	8/2/16		24th 103rd Bde moved forward to 23rd Divisional Area and were attached to 8th Division. Baggage & supply wagons taken. 24th & 25th Bn Northumberland Fusiliers & 208th Field Coy R.E. moved to Forward Area and were attached to 8th Division. 26th & 27th Northumberland Fusiliers moved forward and were attached to 8th Division. LIEUT THOMPSON & LIEUT ADKIN with ½ personnel of No 3 Coy of the Train were attached with 23rd Divisional Train were relieved by Capt W.M. OSBORNE and 2/LT. HARDWICKE with half personnel of No.2 Coy of the Train.	
	9/2/16		10th Lincolns 9/11th Suffolks returned to 31st Divisional Area with baggage and supply wagons. 1 Section for Battery 175 Bde, 1 Section for A&B Batteries 152 Bde, 1 section for Bde 160 Bde 3rd moved to CROIX DU BAC. with baggage and supply wagons.	

1875 Wt. W593/826 1,000,000 4/15 T.R.C. & A. A.D.S.S./Forms/C. 2118.

WAR DIARY or INTELLIGENCE SUMMARY.

Army Form C. 2118.

(Erase heading not required.)

Place	Date	Hour	Summary of Events and Information	Remarks and references to Appendices
BLARINGHEM	11/7/16		Remainder of 175 Bde R.F.A, A&B Batteries 152 Bde, B&D Batteries 160 "B" moved to CROIX DU BAC.	
	13/7/16		102nd By Bde moved to 8th Divisional Area together with 3 Coy of Train and were attached to 8th Division.	
	14/7/16		BRC of 175 Bde RFA, B&C of 160 "B" moved to CROIX DU BAC. Remainder of No 4 Coy of Train moved to 23rd Divl Area and were attached to 23rd Division.	
	15/7/16		"C" Bty 176 B" moved to forward area, and 1 section forming Battery 176, 1 section C&D Battery 152 Bde 1 section for A&C Batteries 160 B" moved to CROIX DU BAC.	
	16/7/16		D&C 152 B" moved to CROIX DU BAC.	
	17/7/16		HQ RE moved to forward area and were attached to 23rd Division.	
	18/7/16		Remainder of 176 Bde RFA, remainder of C&D Batteries 152 Remainder RE Battns 160 & B Bde and BAC 176 moved to forward area.	
	19/7/16		10/21 hy 1 Bde moved to forward area taking baggage, ploughs, wagon.	
	20/9/16		No 2 Coy of Train moved to forward area.	
	21/7/16		H.Q. + No 1 Coy of Train moved to CROIX DU BAC.	
CROIX DU BAC	22/7/16		Railhead LA GORGE. Ryttling Point TROIS ARBRES. 1313 Colonel de 102nd L/6 Bde + No 3 Coy of Train reformed 3rd Division	

Army Form C. 2118.

WAR DIARY
or
INTELLIGENCE SUMMARY.

(Erase heading not required.)

Instructions regarding War Diaries and Intelligence Summaries are contained in F. S. Regs., Part II. and the Staff Manual respectively. Title pages will be prepared in manuscript.

Place	Date	Hour	Summary of Events and Information	Remarks and references to Appendices
CROIX DU BAC	26/4/16		Retiring Point changed to Road running from B.19.d.2.2. to A.18.d.1.3ᵈ Sheet 36.	
	27/4/16		Retiring Point changed to Road from H.3.d.10.2. to H.8.d.1.9. Sheet 36.	

W. Brooke Lt. Col.
Commanding
84th DIVISIONAL TRAIN,
ARMY SERVICE CORPS.

34 Durham

Vol 3

Place	Date	Hour	Summary of Events and Information	Remarks and references to Appendices
CROIX DU BAC	1/3/16 3/3/16		Refilling Point on or about from A22.c.2.8. to A17.c.4.3. Railhead changed to B.A.C. ST. MAUR and refilling done direct from Supply train to Supply wagons of Dvn. Units grouped as follows for purposes of Supplies:- Divisional Troops:- Div. HQ, R.A. HQ, R.E. HQ, Signal Coy R.E., Div Coy Train, Mobile Veterinary Section, Div Cavalry Det (Cyclists, 18th N.F. (Pioneers) 7th Sanitary Section, 176th Bde R.F.A. (inc. Battery) (Corps Troops, 4th Bde R.F.A.):- 118 A.T., 1st Lowland Bde., 1 Section 29th A Coys Bde. (A.T.), 145th Anti aircraft section, 23rd A.A. Section, 39th A.A. Section, 37th A.O. Section, 25th Bde R.F.E., 23rd Regt Bty, 29th Siege Bty, 29th Siege Bty, 30th Siege Bty, 34th Siege Bty, 25th BAC, 34th Am Col. R.F.A., 402nd M.T.W. A.S.C. — 101st Bde Group. Bde HQ (including 1 Sect Signal Coy R.E. & 2 T.M. Bty) 15th Royal Scots, 16th Royal Scots, 10th Lincolns, 11th Suffolks, 207th Coy R.E., 104th Field Ambulance, 152 Bde R.F.A., No 2 Coy Train, Corps Troops:- 20th A.T. Coy R.E., 1 Sect 1st Siege Coy. 102nd Bde Group Bde HQ (including 1 Sect Signal Coy R.E.) 20th North'd Fusiliers, 21st North'd Fusiliers, 22nd North'd Fusiliers, 23rd North'd Fusiliers, 208th Coy R.E., 102nd Field Ambulance, No 2 Coy Train, 175th Bde R.F.A., H.Q.D. Workshops. 103rd Bde Group Bde HQ (including 1 Sect Signal Coy R.E.), 24th North'd Fusiliers, 25th North'd Fusiliers, 26th North'd Fusiliers, 27th North'd Fusiliers, 209th Coy R.E., 103rd Field Ambulance, No 4 Coy Train, 160th Bde R.F.A., No 2 Section 1st Army Siege Pk. H.T. Coy A.D.C., No 6 B.S. M.M.S.	

Army Form C. 2118.

March

WAR DIARY
or
INTELLIGENCE SUMMARY
(Erase heading not required.)

Place	Date	Hour	Summary of Events and Information	Remarks and references to Appendices
CROIX DU BAC	3/3/16		Zones of Refilling :- 101st Bde Group 7.30 am, 102nd Bde Group 8.15 am, 103rd Bde Group 9.0 am, Divl Troops Group 9.45 am.	
	14/3/16		Zones of Refilling :- 103rd Bde Group 7.30 am, 102nd Bde Group 8.15 am, 101st Bde Group 9 am, Divl Troops Group.	
	24.3.16		Division transferred to 2nd Army, 2nd Corps.	

W Evans Lt Col
Comdg 34th Divnl Train

31-3-16

Instructions regarding War Diaries and Intelligence Summaries are contained in F. S. Regs., Part II. and the Staff Manual respectively. Title pages will be prepared in manuscript.

Army Form C. 2118.

"Original"

34 Div Train
Vol 4

WAR DIARY
or
INTELLIGENCE SUMMARY.
(Erase heading not required.)

April 1916

Instructions regarding War Diaries and Intelligence Summaries are contained in F.S. Regs., Part II. and the Staff Manual respectively. Title pages will be prepared in manuscript.

Place	Date	Hour	Summary of Events and Information	Remarks and references to Appendices
CROIX DU BAC	5th		Units of the Division left the forward area for the 2nd Army Reserve Training area as follows:-	
	7th		103rd H/ Bde. and with supply baggage wagons	
			102nd Inf. Bde, 208 & 21 Coy R.E. & No.3 by Divisional Train, Supply wagons from ceding as one convoy, 103rd Fd. Amb.	
	8th		2 Bn 101 Inf Bde, 209 Fd Coy R.E., 104 & 3rd Amb. Supply wagons proceeding as one convoy.	
	9th		18th North'd Fusiliers (Pioneers), 1 Section per A.T, C.D. Batteries, 175 & 152 Bde R.F.A	
	10th		103rd Inf'y Bde, 207 Fd Coy R.E., Divisional Mounted Troops. Remaining Return A.T, C.D. Batteries 175 + 152 Bde. Supply wagons proceeding as one convoy.	
			M.G Coy Divisional Train, 173rd Bde B.A.C	
	11th		101 Inf/ Bde Hrs 2 Bn. One Section per R.B C.D Batteries 160 + 3rd P.F.A Train Hqtr, No 2 & No 4 Coys Divisional Train, Divisional Headquarters	
	12th		Remaining Return 160 & 3rd R.F.A	
	13th		160 Bde B.A.C. M/ g No 1 Section D.A.C.	
	14th		No 2 & 3 Sections D.A.C.	

WAR DIARY
or
INTELLIGENCE SUMMARY.

Army Form C. 2118.

Place	Date	Hour	Summary of Events and Information	Remarks and references to Appendices
SALPERWICK			Divisional Horse Exhibition & Jumping. Headquarters R.21.C.8.2 (27A.S.E.) Div. Coy ½ mile due North of Y in ESQUERDES. No 2 Coy. K.33.d.2.0 (27 A.S.E.) No 3 Coy. J.36.C.6.8 (27A.NE) No 4 Coy. Q.11.C.2.9 (27A.S.E) Railhead WATTEN. Supplies taken by lorry to Refilling Point. Supply Refilling Point now ST. OMER - BOULOGNE RD ½ mile South of R in LUMBRES (HAZEBROUCK 5A)	
	17th	10.0 a.m	Bde troops start Road from Q.11.C.2.2 to 0.6.7. 10.30 a.m 6th Bde troops at R.6.b.7.3	
	27th	10.0 a.m, 10.2 a.m 9.10.3 a.m	Divisional Mounted Troops attached to 2nd Cavalry Division own arrangements for drawing Supplies. Bde Trains took Companies turned over own attacks to their Brigades for purposes of Supplies	

N.S. Monro Lt Col
Comdg 3/4 M.Sm.t. Train

1.5.16

WAR DIARY or INTELLIGENCE SUMMARY

Army Form C. 2118

3rd Divisional Train

Apl. Vol 5

MAY. 1916

Place	Date	Hour	Summary of Events and Information	Remarks and references to Appendices
BALDERWICK	4th		TRAIN Headquarters, Headquarters Company & No.4 Company entrained at ST. OMER for LONGEAU	
	5		No 2 Company of Train entrained at ST. OMER for LONGEAU	
	6th		No 3 Company of Train do do	
			Barges and Supply Wagons of Units of the Division proceeded with the units and met with the Train Companies	
			New Railhead at MERICOURT.	
BEHENCOURT			Train Headquarters at BEHENCOURT; Train Companies erecting Canvas at RIBEMONT. 62 d D27. 6.	
			Refilling Point for the Division situated at roads running from D 27 a 2.9 to D 20 d 8.9. (Sheet 62d).	
	12th		Cyclist Company of Division transferred to 3rd Corps. Existing establishment reduced by 2 drivers & HDhorses, 19 sangers, 13 hooked rough	

Army Form C. 2118

WAR DIARY
or
INTELLIGENCE SUMMARY
(Erase heading not required.)

Instructions regarding War Diaries and Intelligence Summaries are contained in F. S. Regs., Part II. and the Staff Manual respectively. Title Pages will be prepared in manuscript.

Place	Date	Hour	Summary of Events and Information	Remarks and references to Appendices
	26th		Existing Establishment of the Train reduced by 4 G.S. wagons, 4 drivers, and 8 HD horses, owing to reorganisation of Battery and Divisional Ammunition Columns.	
	9th		34th Divisional Cavalry transferred to 7th Corps, reduces establishment of the Train by 3 drivers, 6 HD horses, 3 G.S. wagons	

N.F. Evans .... COMMANDING
34th DIVISIONAL TRAIN,
ARMY SERVICE CORPS.

84 D. Train
Vol 6

Army Form C. 2118.

WAR DIARY
or
INTELLIGENCE SUMMARY.
(Erase heading not required.)

Place	Date	Hour	Summary of Events and Information	Remarks and references to Appendices
BÉHENCOURT	6th		New Railhead at FRECHENCOURT. 33" Reserve Park assisting to convey supplies from Railhead to Dumps.	
	11th		5 G.S. wagons with Sandbagged reserve Rations to BAPAUME BARRIER. Used Tram from Dose to BARRIER.	
	12th		18 G.S. wagons and Limbered G.S. wagons convey Reserve Rations and T.M. ammunition to BAPAUME BARRIER and ammunition to BÉCOURT.	
	13th		6 G.S. wagons to convey Reserve Rations to Artillery Bdes, and 6 G.S wagons convey Sandbagged reserve Rations to BAPAUME BARRIER	
	14th		16 G.S. and 5 Limb. G.S. wagons to convey Bombs to BAPAUME BARRIER. LT. E.W.D. COLT-WILLIAMS A.S.C. detailed as A.S. my representative in charge of the running of the Trains, with 8 men from the Train Resolve News.	
	15th		15 G.S. wagons convey T.M. ammunition to store at HOSPICE and 15 G.S. Wagons to BAPAUME with 2" T.M. Ammunition E118 & Mallard	
	16th		Allotment of Reserve Ration dump and 16 G.S wagons to convey Reserve Rations and Fuel to BAPAUME and BELLEVUE BARN.	
			22 G.S. to convey T.M. ammunition to BAPAUME	
	17th		24 G.S. wagons to convey Reserve Rations to BÉCOURT and ALBERT and 6 G.S. wagons to convey T.M. ammunition to BÉCOURT 12 G.S. wagons with 19th Division Reserve Rations to TRAIN BASE.	
	18th		24 G.S wagons to convey T.M. ammunition from BRESLE to BÉCOURT & 9 G.S with T.M. ammunition from TRAM BASE to BÉCOURT.	
	19th		19 G.S. wagons to convey T.M. ammunition & LEFT KITCHEN DUMP. 20 G.S. wagons to convey & horse reinforcements to 108th etc. and then to convey ammunition etc from TRAM BASE to Trench dumps at BÉCOURT.	
	20th		21 G.S. wagons to convey T.M. ammunition to ALBERT	Continued.

2353 Wt. W3144/1454 700,000 5/15 D.D.&L. A.D.S.S./Forms/C. 2118.

Army Form C. 2118.

WAR DIARY
or
INTELLIGENCE SUMMARY.
(Erase heading not required.)

Instructions regarding War Diaries and Intelligence Summaries are contained in F. S. Regs., Part II. and the Staff Manual respectively. Title pages will be prepared in manuscript.

Place	Date	Hour	Summary of Events and Information	Remarks and references to Appendices
BÉHENCOURT	21st		31 G.S. wagons conveyed gas cylinders to BECOURT and BAPAUME under Major TWEEDY and Capt. SIMPSON.	
	22nd		Move of Railhead to DERMANCOURT. Refilling at E.I.R.C. trading from Train by G.S. wagons. 14 G.S. wagons conveyed gas cylinders to BECOURT and BAPAUME under Major TWEEDY and Capt. SIMPSON	
	23rd		22 G.S. convey T.M. Ammunition to ALBERT and BAPAUME.	
	26th		10 G.S. wagons convey stores to BECOURT, 4 G.S. wagons convey T.M. ammunition to BAPAUME.	
	28th		4 G.S. wagons convey grenades to ALBERT	
	29th		12 G.S. wagons convey stores to BELLEVUE FARM, these failed to get through owing to guide supplied by R.E. taking the wrong road. Double issue of supplies to above System, the 12 loads of Stores sent up again successfully.	
	30th		Divisional Train move from BÉHENCOURT to DERMANCOURT. 10 G.S. wagons of Stores sent to BECOURT. Baggage wagons of Units sent loaded to Train Bivouac in readiness. Casualties among Train horses very low in spite of large amount of extra work done. The R.F.A. Baggage wagons used up more horses than the whole Train. Division complimented by Army, Corps, and Divisional Commanders on the preparatory work carried out. Major W.R. TWEEDY, Capt R. SIMPSON and 2nd Lieut D. MACDONALD were of great assistance to me, but all ranks worked splendidly.	
	10.7.16			

[signature]
COMMANDING
84th DIVISIONAL TRAIN,
ARMY SERVICE CORPS.

E. 118.

Allotment of Reserve Rations.

Divisional Dumps	Rations	Biscuits
LEFT Section	10152	10160
RIGHT Section	10140	10160

Brigade Dumps		
LEFT Brigade	6768	6760
CENTRE Brigade	6768	6760
RIGHT Brigade	6768	6760
Total	40596	40600

Rations are done up in Sandbags. Each Sandbag contains 12 Tins Pres Meat, 12 Iron Grocery Rations, 12 Rations Oxo or Pea Soup, 2 pots of Jam.

Two Sandbags are tied together to make "one man" loads weighing 43 lbs. Biscuits are in 20 lb tins and spare sandbags are dumped with the tins of biscuit.

15-6-16

N. Evans
Lieut Col
C.R.E. 34th Divist France.

34DT909   Secret

Headquarters G.
34th Division

I beg to forward herewith "War Diary" Volume 4, covering the period 1st to 31st July 1916.

3-8-16   [signature]   Lieut. Col.
                                        Commanding
                      84th DIVISIONAL TRAIN,
                      ARMY SERVICE CORPS.

Vol 7

WAR DIARY
or
INTELLIGENCE SUMMARY
(Erase heading not required.)

Army Form C. 2118.

Place	Date	Hour	Summary of Events and Information	Remarks and references to Appendices
	JULY 1916			
DERNANCOURT	1.7.16		2/Lieut D.R. MACDONALD sent to follow up mobile R.F.A. to scout road by which attack up supplies at night. 2/Lt MACDONALD slightly wounded. Supply wagons ready loaded for Bde H.Q. and 1 per Batt. held ready loaded to go up until 10.30 p.m. when it was decided that the transport would prove wagons reading troops before daylight. Attack wagons also held in readiness. Baggage wagons of units loaded and parked with their Train Companies overnight ready to move. 4 G.S. wagons loaded with 50 gallon petrol tins held in readiness at Train BASE. Baggage wagons returned to units at midnight & be off loaded and returned to Train.	
	2.7.16	9 a.m.	Wagons placed at disposal of O.C. Salvage Company	
	3.7.16		8 G.S. wagons with 4 wheelers detailed to take down Tapoulin shelters at BRESLE and were then to FRANVILLERS for wounded	
	4.7.16	9 a.m.	4 G.S. wagons placed at disposal of No Salvage Company 2/Lieut THOMPSON in charge. 5 G.S. wagons placed at disposal of O.C. Salvage Company Lieut HARDWICKE in charge. Baggage wagons returned to units this evening.	
	5.7.16		4 G.S. wagons placed at disposal of Salvage Company daily 9 G.S. wagons attached to D Co. Zetown Battn. Capt. OSBORNE in charge.	

Army Form C. 2118.

WAR DIARY
or
INTELLIGENCE SUMMARY.
(Erase heading not required.)

Instructions regarding War Diaries and Intelligence Summaries are contained in F. S. Regs., Part II. and the Staff Manual respectively. Title pages will be prepared in manuscript.

Place	Date	Hour	Summary of Events and Information	Remarks and references to Appendices
	JULY 1916			
DERNANCOURT	5.7.16	2:30pm	Train Head Quarters moved to BEHENCOURT.	
BEHENCOURT			3 Watertank wagons sent to the Baths at HEHENCOURT. Remainder of Train Bivouac nightly.	
	6.7.16		Nos 1 and 2 companies moved to BAIZIEUX. Refilling Point C 10 b and C 11 a. Railhead FRECHENCOURT. No 3 and 4 companies to 37th Divn now with 102nd and 103rd Brigades. Nos 3 and 4 Companies 37th Division arrive with 111th and 112th Brigades. Transport of 102nd & 113rd Brigades marched under O.C. Train Company. Supply wagons sent separately in order that in time the refill was armed with 37th Division. 6 watertank wagons placed at TRAM BASE and kept holed. Watertank wagons supplied with petrol tins as the circular corrugated tanks proved too weak to stand the bumps on the roads.	
LAVIEVILLE	7.7.16		Train Headquarters and Train Companies moved to LAVIEVILLE. Refilling Point. REFILLING POINT at D 10 d at 1 a.m.	
	9.7.16		LT. D. S. BADDELEY to M.T. School of Instruction ST OMER 3 water wagons to BECOURT DUMP under Lt MICHEL, refilled at BAPAUME DUMP being second trip.	

WAR DIARY
or
INTELLIGENCE SUMMARY

Army Form C. 2118.

Place	Date	Hour	Summary of Events and Information	Remarks and references to Appendices
	JULY 1916			
LAVIEVILLE	9.7.16		8 g.s. wagons to BAPAUME DUMP to do two trips with Reserve rations to SALVAGE STORE ALBERT. 9 waterlank wagons with tankswood and 4 g.s. wagons detailed for permanent duty on Forward Areas. Lt. ADKIN in charge. Four of these detailed for permanent duty under O.C. Salvage Company. Lieut COLT WILLIAMS in charge of Trains.	
	11.7.16		8 g.s. wagons to clear BAPAUME DUMP of Reserve Rations under 2/Lt MACDONALD. Lt. H.G.V. MILLER reported in relief of Lt BADDELEY. Exchange of Nos 2 and 3 Companies with 37th Divl. Train completed so that 1 got back my original companies Nos 231 and 232. CAPT A.R. GODDARD S.O. 101st Bde admitted to Hospital. Railhead to ALBERT.	
	12.7.16		5 g.s. wagons doing ten trips with stone from G DUMP to BECOURT, 2/Lt Macdonald in charge. 5 g.s. wagons at TRAM BASE exchanging for 5 hundred g.s. wagons accounts of fuel found in Forward area.	
	13.7.16		5 g.s. wagons for stones as yesterday 2/Lt BRASSENDEN in charge. 5 g.s. wagons for stone as yesterday 2/Lt HARDWICK E in charge.	

Army Form C. 2118.

WAR DIARY
or
INTELLIGENCE SUMMARY.
(Erase heading not required.)

Place	Date	Hour	Summary of Events and Information	Remarks and references to Appendices
	July 1916			
LAVIÉVILLE	13/7/16		Cards of Honor worked by O.C. 34th Division to No 7th/104075 Pte ANTHONY R.H, No 7th/105051 Pte BIRCH C. No 7th/104511 Pte SPEED T., No 7th/101486 Pte LASTWA, No 7th/113781 Pte HUDSON W. for work at TRAM BASE under LT. E.W.D. COLT WILLIAMS during June and July	
	14/7/16		Railhead to EDGE HILL	
	15/7/16		Supplying of 111th Brigade detailed to take Salvaged stores to ALBERT Railhead daily on their return journey. LT THOMPSON to TRAM BASE in charge of Transport Arr. 5 gs wgns for stores as yesterday. Capt OSBORNE in charge. 2 GS wgns to Tara Dump ALBERT. Fn Veterinary Tram Coopering wgns to LONG VALLE W.20.d.	
	16/7/16		Railhead ALBERT. Relieving by horse transport 2 am. Refilling Point Wood at and after 4 am.	
	17/7/16		5 gs wgns under LT HARRISON to salve Reserve Rations from firewood dumps. 6 gs wgns from storedump in station to BECOURT CEMETERY	
	18/7/16		6 gs wgns from storedump with stores to BECOURT CEMETERY. 8 gs wgns under LT HARRISON to salve Reserve Rations from firewood dumps.	
	19/7/16		6 gs wgns from storedump with stores to BECOURT CEMETERY	

WAR DIARY
or
INTELLIGENCE SUMMARY

Army Form C. 2118.

Place	Date	Hour	Summary of Events and Information	Remarks and references to Appendices
BEHENCOURT	JULY 1916 20/7/16		Train Headquarters moved to BEHENCOURT. Train Companies to BRESLE WOOD	
		3.15am	Drivers McNISH M/1457455 and Lo Laws wounded by shell fire in RUE DES TRAILLES	
			ALBERT after loading at RAILHEAD, one horse killed & shot.	
			Wagons withdrawn from TRAM B & S.E. last night. 4 G.S. wagons detached for permanent duty I.C.C. Salvage Company.	
	21/7/16		Railhead changed to FRECHENCOURT and Supply Column taken into use. Refilling Point D.14 and C.7. am.	
	22/7/16		9 watercart wagons refitted with rectangular tanks. 5 GS wagons detached duty at 5pm to work under C.E. 3 M Coys	
	23/7/16		2 water truck wagons detached duty for B.Hrs at BRESLE until 2 for it. Battn of TRAVELLERS. Remaining 5 used by Train Companies for carrying water to camp.	
	24/7/16		4 GS wagons under Cpl OSBORNE Harry Return watercarts from Salvage duty to Refilling Point as reserve to be reduced to 1 day at 150 rations.	
	25/7/16		Lt HARRISON placed in charge of Remounts and Remedy	
	26/7/16		Buffer wagons returned to Train	

WAR DIARY
or
INTELLIGENCE SUMMARY.
(Erase heading not required.)

Army Form C. 2118.

Place	Date	Hour	Summary of Events and Information	Remarks and references to Appendices
	July 1916			
BERENCOURT	29.7.16	9 pm	2/Lt MacDONALD in charge of rations left with sand bags and rations for LONELY COPSE DUMP & MAMETZ. Enroute, experienced great difficulty owing to shell hits in road.	
M.30.d	30.7.16		Train Halgarten and Train Engineer wood & LONELY VALLEY Wood	
	31.7.16		Refilling Pt Horse Transport for Train at ALBERT Railhead at 11.30pm Refilling Point EMERGENCY ROAD N°3 at W.27 and left at 2am	
	3rd August 1916			

Signature
COMMANDING
84th DIVISIONAL TRAIN.
ARMY SERVICE CORPS.

34D/T986   SECRET

Headquarters G.
34th Division

I beg to forward herewith War Diary, Volume No 8, covering period 1st to 31st August 1916.

1-9-16.

                                     Lieut Col
                                     COMMANDING
                              84th DIVISIONAL TRAIN,
                              ARMY SERVICE CORPS.

Army Form C. 2118.

Vol 8

WAR DIARY
or
INTELLIGENCE SUMMARY.
(Erase heading not required.)

Instructions regarding War Diaries and Intelligence Summaries are contained in F. S. Regs., Part II. and the Staff Manual respectively. Title pages will be prepared in manuscript.

Place	Date	Hour	Summary of Events and Information	Remarks and references to Appendices
W.20d ALBERT Central Shed	1.8.16		Railhead ALBERT. Refilling Point on EMERGENCY ROAD No 3 at W.2 at 2am. Loading by horse transport at Railhead at 11.30 p.m. Train arr. badly placed so that I had to break wagons on to 5 tracks reported number 3rd Inf. The trains are still at the Railhead. Sent 4992 rations with 53 to the Brigades to MAMETZ DUMP & to BRUSSENDEN in charge of 6 wagons. 4 wagons working daily under OC Salvage Co. The money order took wagons sent to 112th Brigade were sent hospital to 3 artillery wagons. Not being detailed supply working rations to the Train. Hung. T. M. Batteries & M.V.S.	
	2.8.16		Loading and Refilling service as yesterday. 3 G/S wagons for Salvage from MAMETZ & LONELY COPSE	
	3.8.16		Refilling attempt place at 2 am. Loading at ALBERT RAILHEAD at 3 am. Train late in coming in so that Refilling did not start till 5 am. Lieut COLT-WILLIAMS placed in charge of LONELY COPSE DUMP. 3 GS wagons to work under CRE from F4&7.b. C.S.M. CLARKE A/C S. M. sent for Salvage from MAMETZ & LONELY COPSE. There are in addition to the 4 wagons working daily under OC Salvage Company	

T.2134. Wt. W708-776. 500000. 4/15. Sir J. C. & S.

Army Form C. 2118.

WAR DIARY
or
INTELLIGENCE SUMMARY.
(Erase heading not required.)

Instructions regarding War Diaries and Intelligence Summaries are contained in F. S. Regs., Part II. and the Staff Manual respectively. Title pages will be prepared in manuscript.

Place	Date	Hour	Summary of Events and Information	Remarks and references to Appendices
N 20 d ALBERT Central start	4.8.16	7	7 limbered wagons under Lt. BLACKBURN sent to LONELY COPSE DUMP to turn this and work up loads and ammunition as required. Arrived with R.S.O. to endure wagons when to load at Railhead on Train is centrally late. It arrived today at 5.30 a.m. Refilled at 11 a.m. 6 wagons under Lt. MILLER working under C.R.E. from G. Dump to MAMETZ. 4 wagons for salvage from MAMETZ to LONELY COPSE.	
	5.8.16		Train guns late. Refilling took place about 8 a.m. 4 wagons for salvage from MAMETZ to LONELY COPSE.	
	6.8.16		Train late. Railhead at 5 a.m. refilling at 6 a.m. 4 wagons for salvage from MAMETZ to LONELY COPSE. 1 waterwagon to 112th Brigade barrage by shell fire but water cart which it is being if in use.	
	7.8.16		Carted at 4 a.m. ALBERT thoroughly shelled but a K.C. gunner the station. 2nd Refilling at 5 p.m. 4 p. wagons for salvage from MAMETZ to LONELY COPSE	

WAR DIARY
or
INTELLIGENCE SUMMARY

Army Form C. 2118.

Place	Date	Hour	Summary of Events and Information	Remarks and references to Appendices
W.20.d	7.8.16		The lorries dumped supplies for tomorrow's refilling in front of Company HQ, map square at 9.30 p.m.	
ALBERT				
Cul-de-sac	8.8.16		Railhead MERICOURT. Refilling at 4 a.m. Lorries dumped at midday	
	9.8.16		Refilling as yesterday. Lorries dumped at midday	
	10.8.16		Refilled 112th Brigade at midnight, so as to enable the first line Transport to pick their stores in coming up. The supplies as they had been only brought skilled otherwise arrangements as yesterday.	
		2.30 p.m.	Lent to No 207 GRE. motor lorries.	
			Refilled 112th Brigade at 6 p.m. today. Tr. Ermencourt. [illegible] men were killed when passing through (ALBERT or [illegible]) but no casualties	
	11.8.16		Refilling as yesterday	
		3.0 p.m.	[illegible] Lieut. MICHEL to CRE to carry sand bags to [illegible]	
	12.8.16		Refilling as yesterday. Railhead at FRECHENCOURT	
	13.8.16		Refilling as yesterday. Church service and Holy Communion held in Camp at 6 p.m.	
	14.8.16		Brigade major attended to meals for men. Refilling as yesterday. Railhead at MERICOURT	

Army Form C. 2118.

WAR DIARY
or
INTELLIGENCE SUMMARY.
(Erase heading not required.)

Place	Date	Hour	Summary of Events and Information	Remarks and references to Appendices
BEHENCOURT	15.8.16		Refilled at W20d at 8am. Train Coys Nos 2, 3, 4 went to BRESLE. Train HQ at BEHENCOURT.	
	16.8.16		No 1 Company left W20d as the Artillery had not moved yet. Railhead to FRECHENCOURT. Refilled on BAIZIEUX—FRANVILLERS Road at 8am and at 3pm as transport marched on 17th with infantry between an 18#y tactical train, so 2 hap supplies have to be railed to unit today. I carted the road to HALLENCOURT. Run for water easier.	
CARDONNETTE	17.8.16		Visited M.T.O. Train and C.R.A. Re arrangements respecting the ATA at Divisn Amm stn. 2/Lt CLEGEMAN's placed in command of all the transport. Transport on the march divided into 4 groups. No1 group in charge of Capt L J MURPHY R.F.; No2 group 2/Lt H.J.T. MAYNE A.S.C. No 3 group i/c Capt L.J. MURPHY R.F.; No 4 group i/c Capt H.B. COMBE A.P.M. Starting points with attached. All groups to marched their billeting places Feuy 20.17 & 18 #J by Lynn and refilling of troops carrying out in 20 completed by 7pm	hand copy attached

Place	Date	Hour	Summary of Events and Information	Remarks and references to Appendices
HALLENCOURT	13.8.16		The No 1 group marched off at 5.30 a.m. All 3 groups taking part by 7.30 a.m. In spite of No 2 group not having moved to Tangry at 9. Whilst Staff Regt that had arrived later has only one lorry & lbs delay at level crossing at PICQUIGNY, arr. HANGEST and LONGPRÉ. Early all groups during LONGPRÉ had convoy at bridge. Watered mass to No 1 group at CROUY, No 2 group at ST PIERRE, No 3 L.N.A. group East of PIRANCOURT	7.40
	17.8.16		Reported at Headquarters No 11 Bgde at DUNCQ. Fr. 11 Bgde Smith Signal Co, of KN Staffs, REC, present. FAKROU, 11th NF, MERE LES ART F.1/2 Bgde 1 mile North of BETTENCOURT at T and Railhead HANGEST. Met — a QR. RT. RV and afternoon took to mess. LT LEIGH Toll Supply Officer for artillery group last billet to find R.A. Headquarters 5.30 moved on to BAC ST MAUR area	
DOULIEU	18.8.16		Reported at 9 a.m. at DUNCQ for instructions after moving by ____ from PONTREMY and 1st Train load to North of BETTENCOURT for the issue of LUNSPE Battalion trains and supply my ordered. proceeded by Car to BAC ST MAUR area, Billet at DOULIEU	

WAR DIARY
or
INTELLIGENCE SUMMARY.
(Erase heading not required.)

Army Form C. 2118.

Place	Date	Hour	Summary of Events and Information	Remarks and references to Appendices
DIVLIEU	21.8.16		Received B+C St MAUR. Supply Columns No 18 Division	
			Refilling Point 101st Brigade & Mark Staff, 102nd Field Amb. H.I.C. 5.B. 86.136	
			111th Brigade, 103rd Field Amb, Div HQ Signal Co, R.E. HQ 112 Bde and 112th 40.5 pp	
			M.G.Co at G.19.d.58. — 11 a.m.	
	22.8.16		Refilling Point 111th Bde group at district H.I.C. 5.3. 111th Bde from 3rd G. R.E.	
			Dt Div & C.R.E. at G.26.d.3.4. 5th 111th Brigade 2 of A.R.E. 102nd & 103rd	
			Field Amb & Div HQ Signal Co Supply point at G. 19.d.58	
			No 3 Conference ground R 6.6.6.6.	
			111th & 112th Bde with 9th Mark Staff and Inf regrouped 37 Division	
			102nd and 103rd Brigades with 18th Mark Staff and inf regrouped 34th Division.	
			Considerable part of the transport went by road in medium sized	
			trains THOMPSON that day doing back traffic in ⸺ return to	
			transport for 2nd day train & Verry & B.2.4.4.4.M.E.	
	23.8.16		Refilling at 11 a.m. as above - refilling 102nd 103rd Brigades 18th W.S.St.,	
			111th and 112th Bdes - 19 M.C. Staff R.f.t. Artillery regrouped - G.A.T	
	24.8.16		Refilling at 11 a.m. as on 23.8.16. Div HQ moved to ORAILOND + C	

War Diary or Intelligence Summary

Army Form C. 2118.

Place	Date	Hour	Summary of Events and Information	Remarks and references to Appendices
DOULIEU	24.8.16		Lieut THOMPSON attached to K Baggage from 37th Division at once with 162 LT & 103rd Bde left at 4am. Arranged Supply trans to meet 103rd Brigade to III Corps Transferred 2 HD from N62 to N646 in order to join 34th Div's 2 Coys. Arranged to loan lorry to North Transport from Railhead for temporary service	
CROIX DU BAC	25.8.16		Loaded at Railhead B.t.CE ST MAUR. H.T. fr 34 Corps 10.15 & 10.25. Bdes Lorries loaded for 103rd Bde for diestick stores in refilling at 11 am, 2nd at 2.30pm so that supply waggons return loaded from 5 group of men N63 Cy to escort 103rd Bde. 15 Gs wagons used in afternoon to move coke & charcoal from Railhead to Carsbury. Train HT Bayard & CROIX DU BAC.	
	26.8.16		Loaded at Railhead in extends the same Refilling at 10.30am 350 mut am with Capt Shelton Inspector of century.	
	27.8.16 to 31.8.16		Railhead B.t.C ST MAUR. Loading by Horse Transport at 8am. Refilling at same Refilling Points at 10.30am.	

1.9.16

N.J. Evansktock
Comdg 34 H.Transport Column

34DT 65/A   SECRET

Headquarters G.
34th Division.

    I beg to forward herewith "War Diary" Volume 9 covering the period 1st to 30th Sept 1916.

[signature]

5-10-16

Lieut Col COMMANDING
34th DIVISIONAL TRAIN,
ARMY SERVICE CORPS.

WAR DIARY
INTELLIGENCE SUMMARY

Army Form C. 2118.

Vol 9

Place	Date	Hour	Summary of Events and Information	Remarks and references to Appendices
SEPTEMBER 1916				
CROIX DU BAC	1.9.16		Railhead BAC ST MAUR. Entering by Horse Transport at 8 am. Refilling at 10.30 am as follows. Divisional Troops at G.18 b 7.2. 101st Brigade at C.10.7.8.; 102nd Brigade at B.26 d.3.4. Supply Column 96.18.	Ref Sheet 36
	2.9.16		No 2 Company moved to G.3 c 1.9.	
	4.9.16		New Zealand Supply Column replaces No 18 Divisional Supply Column.	
			No 1 Company moved to FROID NID FERME at A.26 d 1.9.	
			No 3 Company moved to G.2 d 5.3.	
	7.9.16		Refilling Points moved for 101st Brigade to G.4 C	
			102nd Brigade to G.10 a	
	8.9.16		No change in R.A.T.illery until R.F.A. wagon lines came back. Covered draught from the Barges which have been drawn Oats have suffered considerably from hydration of grease.	
	14.9.16		Refilling Point for R.A. changed to A.27 b 5.0. Time 10.30 am	
	22.9.16		103rd Brigade and No 4 Company of the train separated the Division. No 4 Company in billets and bivouac at G.2 b 58.	
	23.9.16		Refilling Point for 103rd Brigade at H.9 b 4.8.	

WAR DIARY
or
INTELLIGENCE SUMMARY.
(Erase heading not required.)

Army Form C. 2118.

Place	Date	Hour	Summary of Events and Information	Remarks and references to Appendices
SEPTEMBER 1916				
CROIX DU BAC	30.9.16		From 7.9.16 all available wagons being used for carrying bricks from nightly houses in Fromelles area for the construction of Hutstandings. All spare time occupied in making clothing and preparing for winter. MT. lorry being be busier averaging 1 to 13 miles per day	
	5.10.16			

[signature]
COMMANDING
34th DIVISIONAL TRAIN,
ARMY SERVICE CORPS.

34DT 138/A

SECRET

Headquarters "G",
34th Division

I beg to forward herewith "War Diary" Volume 10 covering the period 1st to 31st October 1916.

[signature]
Lieut Col COMMANDING
34th DIVISIONAL TRAIN,
ARMY SERVICE CORPS.

1.11.16

Army Form C. 2118.

Vol 10

WAR DIARY
or
INTELLIGENCE SUMMARY.
(Erase heading not required.)

Place	Date	Hour	Summary of Events and Information	Remarks and references to Appendices
CROIX DU BAC	1.10.16		Railhead BAC ST MAUR. Supply Column loads up horse Transport employed in drawing supplies from Railhead. The supply wagons of the Train Allocated to Railhead by formations and proceed direct to refilling points where loads are shifted and supplies issued to units. Refilling Point G at A 27 h 50 to 54 for Divisional Troops G 4 c M 7.0 ,, ,, 101st Brigade G 10 a 7.5 ,, 102nd Brigade H 9 a 4.5 ,, 103rd Brigade H 4 h 3.0 & 3.3 Refilling Point for 103rd Brigade changed to A 4 h 3.0 & 3.3 on 29th. Returning the horses were halted conveniently near Conferences held as follows: No 1 Company at A 21.d.2.10 No 2. Company at C 3.c.1.9 No 3. Company at A 21.A.4.1 No 4 Company at C 2.b.7.8 All spare time employed in turning stables and putting harness	Reference Sheet 36

WAR DIARY or INTELLIGENCE SUMMARY

Army Form C. 2118.

Place	Date	Hour	Summary of Events and Information	Remarks and references to Appendices
CROIX DU BAC	19/10/16		Had startling, erecting cook house, forges etc	
	20/10/16		No 2 Company at all horses under cover & it had standing and was full staff in a barn	
	21/10/16		No 3 Company got all horses under cover but standing and men in barn	
	23/10/16		No 4 Company got all horses under cover and had standing under to get men into barns & stables and not started by the frame until 27.10.16	
	26/10/16		No 1 Company got half of horses and men in and standing for the other as ordered by 15th of this month	
	4.10.16		A Special Batt was created in town at GHQ 6.9 the town this Drawing was constructed in & soldiers marching being attached from Drummond (B.M.) of ERPINGHAM. Captain in charge of Captain CARNES R.M.C. M.O. & Town and R.A.M. lighting of the Animal of the town, R.A. and infantry Major Allan Iches commenced on A.W 16	

Place	Date	Hour	Summary of Events and Information	Remarks and references to Appendices
CROIX DU BAC			During the month was all 3 Coys also known on the lines all [illegible] Coys were employed in & still to takes the long [illegible] and [illegible] also the other camouflaged completions to Security of material which was employed from 17.10.16 to [illegible] the supply of bricks + R.E. [illegible] twenty a long hindrance of it. Not three abuses of mirrors in Sleeps are from the town of LA MOTTE and are 2-3 M.	

31.10.16

[signature]

34 DT 248/A   SECRET

Headquarters
34th Division G

    I beg to forward herewith "War Diary" volume No XI covering the period 1st to 30th November 1916.

3-12-16   [signature] Lieut Colonel COMMANDING
34th DIVISIONAL TRAIN,
ARMY SERVICE CORPS.

WAR DIARY
or
INTELLIGENCE SUMMARY

Army Form C. 2118.

34 D Train

Vol XI

Place	Date	Hour	Summary of Events and Information	Remarks and references to Appendices

CROIX DU BAC	1.11.16		Railhead BAC ST MAUR. Supply columns loaded up, have brought employed to dumps of supplies to Railhead. Supply dump of the Division now in bulk at Railhead by Division personnel & the Refilling Points when detail were issued out.
			
			Refilling Points at A27d 5.0 & 5.4 for Divl Troops
			   G 4 c 7.0 " 101st Brigade
			   G 10 a 7.5 " 102nd Brigade
			   H A b 3.0 & 3.3 " 103rd Brigade
			
			Train companies billetted as follows
			  No1 Company at A 26 d 8.10
			  No 2 — — G 3 c 1.9
			  No 3 — — G 2 d 4.1
			  No 4 — — G 2 b 7.8
				Refer Sketch

	10.11.16		No1 Company completed the making of its stabling. No new horses were available & not general shelter into plank & iron buildings through the saw mill to rent makeshift for an recognised as a	

WAR DIARY
or
INTELLIGENCE SUMMARY

(Erase heading not required.)

Place	Date	Hour	Summary of Events and Information	Remarks and references to Appendices
CROIX DU BAC	10.11.16		a billet and then practices	
	15.11.16		No more critical would be for the Front but lines belong to so unusuable to find out how much road state.	
	22.11.16		The Corps Commander Lt.Gen Sir A.J. GODLEY K.C.B. K.C.M.G. inspected the two lotte lines and expressed satisfaction with the condition	
	29.11.16		Maj Gen Russell comdg New Zealand Division inspected the boards of fascines with Divisional Comments	
	29.11.16		Refilling Point for 103rd Bde. by arrangements Cyclist 3.8. Areous the Brigade had been relieved by the Unity 3rd Australian Division and had moved to dugouts in 34 Kilometre Area	

3.12.16

M.J. Burns Lt.Col.
Comdg 3rd N.Z. (Rifle) Brigade

34DT405/A   <u>SECRET</u>

Headquarters
34th Division G.

    I beg to forward herewith "War Diary" volume No 12 covering the period 1st to 31st December 1916.

                     [signature] Major

12-1-17

WAR DIARY or INTELLIGENCE SUMMARY

Army Form C. 2118

Original

34 Div Train

Vol / 2

Place	Date	Hour	Summary of Events and Information	Remarks and references to Appendices
CROIX DU BAC	**DECEMBER** 1-12-16	—	Horse standings, stables, and stable sheds completed, with the exception of No 2 Co., who have not got much preparations for horses of baggage wagons. The necessary bricks and cinders are not at present available for this purpose.	
"	2-12-16	—	Lieut. R.D. MILLIGAN joined the Train, and posted to No. 3 Co. as transport subaltern.	
"	18-12-16	—	Forage ration of animals in 2nd Army fixed at the following scale:— *(horses plough)*	2nd A.R.O. No. 5-32 f 18-12-16

Class A (working draft)
	Oats	Hay	Straw
	18 lbs	8 lbs	5 lbs

Class B (Ammunition park)
	Oats	Hay	Straw
	17 lbs	8 lbs	5 lbs

Officers chargers & other horses one 13 hands & over	14	8	5
Cobs	10	6	2
		13	8
		8	6
Large mules	12	8	2
		10	
Small mules	6	6	2
		6	

About 50% of the Artillery horses are under Class B, as a substantial saving in forage is effected.

| | 22/12/16 | — | Surprise inspection by Commander in Chief. Train represented by a detachment under Major W.R. TWEEDIE. | |
| | 23/12/16 | — | Christmas Day. Canteen profits without of private Christmas dinners for the men, who all enjoyed themselves thoroughly and no crime whatsoever. | |

WAR DIARY or INTELLIGENCE SUMMARY

Army Form C. 2118.

Place	Date	Hour	Summary of Events and Information	Remarks and references to Appendices
CROIX DU BAC	DECEMBER 27/12/16	—	Lt. Col. E.E. EVANS, O.C. Train, proceeds on 10 days leave. Major R. STUDDERT assumes temporary command.	
"	28/12/16	—	Letter received from Colonel R. SIMPSON, O.C. No 2 Company, on leave in CANADA, to say that his leave is extended from 27th Dec. to 15th January, pending decision as to whether he will be transferred to Canadian Army.	
"	29/12/16	—	Capt. ATHERTON and Bn/M. CARR SCOTT, RAVC and O.C. Company inspected by S.P. Divisional Train (T.F.), arrived from England for 6 days course of instruction. Colonel ATHERTON attached to Train Headquarters and Capt. Gregson to No 1 Company.	
"	31/12/16	—	During the month Train horses have been employed in the material to material at Steenwerck every evening. Issues of reserve supply delivery 4 and 14 — Observation and work have been carried on by the Train to the requirements published in the Back Area Supply Officers' instructions for action on the supply of b.c. to the various sections, loading & return convergence by mail.	

Mitchell Major RA
O.C. 3rd Divisional Train

11-1-17.

34 DIV TRAIN Vol/3

WAR DIARY
or
INTELLIGENCE SUMMARY
(Erase heading not required.)

Army Form C. 2118.

Place	Date	Hour	Summary of Events and Information	Remarks and references to Appendices
CROIX-DU-BAC	Nov 7		Capt BRYAN admitted to No 1 Field Ambulance and passed on to No 2 C.C.S. Bailleul	
"	8		Capt MAYNE attached to 2nd Field Coy 1st Reserve Station	
"	9		Colonel ATHERTON and GREGSON, S.D.2 Liaison, return to England	
"	"		Captain BRYAN return to duty from Casualty Clearing Station	
"	"		No. 1 horse-spare ammunition for transport to 301 Company. 2 crews admitted to M.V.R. sick division in wire screens (incomplete) from a preventive department.	
"	"		Received official intimation that WWI RAILWAYS has been granted an extension of leave to the War Office, pending arrival of a sachet board.	
"	10		Supply Train unable to come on to BAC St MAUR owing to last column to have gone over there owing to L.R. St MAUR owing to L.R.O. to have working of LA BOBQUE (?) at 2.30 p.m. — Convoy was remarkably speedy and steady of Station at 4.30 p.m. This speed of the practicability of always starting at railhead at any rate in the event of the last division of trains, as an emergency. On immediate leaving of trains, labour of Hempstead would be affected of this was attended.	
"	12		2nd Army Commander (Genl PLUMER) accompanied by DAKAR.G Divisional ?? and G.O.C. 30 Sep. inspected Transport Lines of the Division, and No 4 Company of the Train. Genl ? with the Company General — Recommended purchase of sharpening machines for Steward Clipper —	

WAR DIARY
or
INTELLIGENCE SUMMARY.
(Erase heading not required.)

Army Form C. 2118.

Vol XIII

Place	Date	Hour	Summary of Events and Information	Remarks and references to Appendices
CROIX DU BAC	January 1917 13th	—	Drew 8 wagon loads of Bricks from HOUPLINES during the night. The Bricks will be used the make standings for the 2 Company baggage horses. Horses completing the horse standings for the wagon Train.	
"	14th		103rd M.G. Company have the Division for temporary duty at CAESTRE, accompanied by its Supply wagon. Period of schemes interior Reorganization of Divisional Artillery, to be carried out as follows:— (1) 175. B.d. (How 2 Battery) become dated 21-12-16, carried out and completed as follows:— (1) 175. B.d. (How 2 Battery) become an Army Field Artillery Brigade, remaining attached to this division. (2) One section C/175 to join B D/152 and the other section of C/175 of D/110 B.d. to bring these batteries & one section of a six gun establishment. (3) No 3 Section D.A.C. becomes 175th F.A.B.d. Amm Col, remaining attached to 34th D.A.C. (4) No 4 Section D.A.C. will now be numbered No 3 Section, 34th D.A.C. "B" Echelon 34th D.A.C. Train transport affected as follows:— 7 wagons together with 3 extra forage wagons transferred with (175.B.d) to A.F.A.B.d. D.A.C., together with a further 3 extra forage wagons transferred to A.F.A.B.d.. 2 wagons belonging to C/175 B.d. (howitzer) became surplus, the reason of the eventually transferred or evacuated as a complete "Turn out" (wagons that supplies horses may be absorbed to complete wanting deficiencies).	

Army Form C. 2118.

WAR DIARY
or
INTELLIGENCE SUMMARY.
(Erase heading not required.)

Place	Date	Hour	Summary of Events and Information	Remarks and references to Appendices
CROIX DU BAC	January 1917 14th (Contd.)		These reductions will leave the Train with only 14 extra forage wagons instead of 20; and, as no extra transport is allowed for the increased strength of the two R.A. Brigades left with the Division, it is probable that some overloading will be necessitated. — [Attempts for Redistribution of Train Transport:— B.M.B. 9/5972 (A.A.1.) dated 28-12-16.] A device for carrying water for horses in two 4-gall. petrol cans fixed under the seat of all R.S. Wagons is received from D.H.Q., with instructions to have it fitted in a Train wagon, for subsequent inspection by Corps. 20 I.W. instructed to carry out the work. — Instructions with the object of reducing road traffic during a Thaw, issued by D.H.Q. —	
"	15th		3 days forage for Division to be dumped at various places during the hard frost, and only to be made use of when Thaw restrictions are ordered — D.H.Q. decide to have the forage dumped by M.T. at 7 separate places, near the various transport lines, and delivered to units at once, and so save all forage transport during the Thaw.— Also to have ordinary Refilling for Brigade Groups on the BAC ST MAUR – ERQUINGHEM road, during Thaws, and so save backward & forward Traffic between Railhead & present Refilling Points.— R.A. dump to remain unchanged for ordinary supplies.— Proposed sites for forage dumps submitted to D.H.Q. and approved.—	

Army Form C. 2118.

WAR DIARY
or
INTELLIGENCE SUMMARY.
(Erase heading not required.)

Place	Date	Hour	Summary of Events and Information	Remarks and references to Appendices
CROIX DU BAC	January 1919			
	16th		Grocery truck of supply train failed to arrive B&C 8° MAUR, owing to late departure from CALAIS. Arrange to have contents of truck drawn from LA CORGUE by M.T. and motors. Refilling until 12.30 p.m.	
"	17th		In reply to query by D.D. Remounts, through D.H.R., as to number of H.D. Horses which will be found surplus after reorganisation of R.A., point that the 4 horses shown surplus according to establishment can be absorbed in the Train, which is deficient of 8 H.D., therefore no horses will be actually surplus.	
"	18th		Report wagons now fitted with devices for carrying water. Take this men on low to fit, and can be done by unskilled labor. Difficult to obtain serviceable four gallon petrol cans, as that size of can is not now being issued. Forward tabular statement of D.H.R. showing in detail how Train Transport is affected by Reorganisation of Artillery.	Appendices A & B attached
"	19th		Report road water-carrying devices requested by A.A.&Q.M.G., 34th Division, who agrees that there is a serious objection to it in that the dead loads on the cars when there are two men on the box, owing to the lightness of the springs, tends to [...] Nevertheless this it be best for a month to test the efficiency of the new Provisions as to the fitting system for of H-motor lorries.	

2353 Wt.W2544/1454 700,000 5/15 D.D.&L. A.D.S.S./Forms/C. 2118.

Army Form C. 2118.

WAR DIARY
or
INTELLIGENCE SUMMARY.
(Erase heading not required.)

Instructions regarding War Diaries and Intelligence Summaries are contained in F. S. Regs., Part II. and the Staff Manual respectively. Title pages will be prepared in manuscript.

Place	Date	Hour	Summary of Events and Information	Remarks and references to Appendices
CROIX DU BAC	January 1919 19th		Orders received for Lieut. A.E.A. LEE, R.O. Divisional Troops, and Divisional Claims Officer, to report to D.D.S.T. 2nd Army, with Interpreter, Clerk, and Car, for duty on "Demonvers" with the 2nd Army Purchasing Board on 22nd January. — A protest was lodged by D.H.B., owing to shortage of Effective Officers in the Train, but was overruled by Army. —	
"	20th		Telegram received to "Prepare Three Precautions." — Only two days forage to be drawn instead of three. — Fuel to be treated in the same manner. — Oats not being available at Field Supply Depot, only one days oats and two days Hay will actually be issued. — Five particulars of Forage dumps to S.C.S.O., and sent instructions to Officers commanding Companies and Supply Officers. — Owing to reduced quantity of forage to be handled and convenient positions of dumps it will be possible for the Train wagons to remove all the forage from dumps to transport lines during the afternoon. —	
"	21st		Arrangements re Three Precautions, as above, carried out with complete success. — Also units for 3 days fuel given to every unit, with instructions to draw at once. —	
"	22nd		Extra days oats now available, so drawn and issued at Refilling Point. — Every unit now in possession of 2 days forage and 3 days fuel, making Three Precautions complete from A.S.C. standpoint. —	

WAR DIARY or INTELLIGENCE SUMMARY

Army Form C. 2118.

Place	Date	Hour	Summary of Events and Information	Remarks and references to Appendices
CROIX DU BAC	January 14/17 22nd		Lieut. A.I.H. Kee departs for Headquarters 2nd Army to take up his duties with the Army Purchasing Board, in accordance with D.D.S.S. letter No. S/7/21/2/16 of 15/1/15. Receive information that Lt. Col. E.G. Evans is to be returned home as the result of a Medical Board, and Major (Temp Lieut. Colonel) A.W. ALEXANDER has been ordered to take command of the Train —	
"	23rd		Wagon with water-carrying device fitted, inspected by A.D.M.S. 2nd ANZAC, who decides that it is worth trying in spite of the fact that the new gills on the petrol cans when two men on the box — He directs a weeks trial of the device, with the cans full of water on an ordinary working wagon — Report all these precautions now complete to D.H.Q.	
	24th		Captain MAYNE rejoins the Train from Base Hospital —	
	25th		Lt. Col. A.W. ALEXANDER arrives, and takes over command of the Train from Major R. STUDDERT —	
	26th		Orders received for the Division (less Artillery) to move to METEREN — CAESTRE District on the 27th. Move to be completed by mid-day. Orders issued to the Train Companies accordingly.	

WAR DIARY or INTELLIGENCE SUMMARY.

(Erase heading not required.)

Army Form C. 2118.

Place	Date	Hour	Summary of Events and Information	Remarks and references to Appendices
	January 1917			
CROIX DU BAC	26th	—	Supplies for 27th had already been delivered when orders arrived. All Supply & Baggage waggons were sent to Estruito - Reserve M.T. for "Shaw Recaution" was collected into one Group and 6 Guard mounted. Duel Dump handed over to 6 N.Z. Batt. Train.	
FLÊTRE	27th	—	Divisen housed. Supplies housed at B.A.C. S.T. MAUR into M.T. Refilling at 1 p.m. in rear Brigade Area. Refilling was complete by 4 p.m. but owing to slippery nature of Roads it was decided to speed up the train between CAESTRE Road in future. Informed that CAESTRE would be Railhead on the 29th inst. Duel for the train from N.Z. Division.	
	28th		The following orders for moves on 15th-29th received. 24 Fld Br: N.F. to TATINGHEM 2 " " " - } 18 " " " - } MOULLE 207 & 209 Cos R.E. } 3rd Army Area. Arrangements were made for supplying these units.	

Army Form C. 2118.

WAR DIARY
or
INTELLIGENCE SUMMARY.
(Erase heading not required.)

Place	Date	Hour	Summary of Events and Information	Remarks and references to Appendices
	January 1917			
FLÊTRE	28th		Refitting of CAESTRE Horse & Motor Transport except for R.A. which was to be by M.T. in future.	
	29th		Supply Train very late, no units leaving the Division were refilled from No. 2. F.S.D. A.S.C. collected Reserves of forage left at CROIX DU BAC no fod in position, but little or more was found in some cases. Report rendered as to which Units had not complied with instructions given.	
	30th		Salvage Office collected at Reserve Fuel from BRUIGNHEM ek. entrained at FLÊTRE. sent it to fuel Dump at FLÊTRE.	
	31st		Fuel arrived on Supply Train — leaved drawn from N.Z. Divn.	A.W. Alexander Lt. Col. O/C 34th Divl. Train

"ORIGINAL"

Army Form C. 2118.

WAR DIARY
or
INTELLIGENCE SUMMARY.

(Erase heading not required.)

34 D. to Trains

Place	Date	Hour	Summary of Events and Information	Remarks and references to Appendices
	February 1917			
FLÊTRE	1st	—	1st Corps orders issue to units of 2 days Iron Reserve forage. Lt.Adj: Hardwicke admitted to Hospital. Duties of Adjutant taken over.	
	2nd	—	103rd Bde (less 24th & 25th Bns R.F.) 103rd Field Ambulance & No. 4 Coy. Train ordered to move to Training Area tomorrow — Rations for 4th to be taken in Supply Wagons. Afternoon breakdown from ST OMER. Supply Train kept very late — the morning mail were too from	
F.D.	3rd	—	CAESTRE.	
	4th	—	Issue of Reserve Forage to Units commenced. Orders received for Lieut. Coll. Williams 15th to be attached for 10 days to a Battery in the Line y Thereafter to H.Q.'s (Q) for 1 month.	
	5th	—	Issue of Reserve forage completed. 2 Surplus wagons handed over to 25th Divn. Drew Remounts from BAILLEUL Station. 8 for Train — 7 for Men units separated from the Division. Remounts distributed - 6 for 103rd B.R.C. sent to RENESCURE.	
	6th	—		
	7th	—	All leave stopped.	

"ORIGINAL"

Army Form C. 2118.

WAR DIARY
or
INTELLIGENCE SUMMARY.

(Erase heading not required.)

Instructions regarding War Diaries and Intelligence Summaries are contained in F. S. Regs., Part II. and the Staff Manual respectively. Title pages will be prepared in manuscript.

Place	Date	Hour	Summary of Events and Information	Remarks and references to Appendices
FLÊTRE	11th Feb.		Inspected new device for carrying water in G.S. Wagon. Twice enclosed in Biscuit Box with seal. Disadvantages. The Box called Driver's Knees & neutralises spring. New commenced. No: 3. Coy: 1 Horse evacuated sick, dead.	
	12th		Lieut: COLT-WILLIAMS to a Battery in the Line for Training. No: 4 Coy: 1 Horse died. 1st D.S.C. move to CAESTRE	
	13th		No: 3 Sec: DAC & ½ R.A. H.Qrs. move to HAZEBROUCK	
	15th		Operation orders for move of Division South on 18th & 19th received	
	16th		Orders received to "Impose Shaw Restrictions"	
	17th		No: 1 Coy: refill at ERQUINGHEM - and to Shaw Restrictions - later to interfere with move of Division. 102nd Bde. refill later & supply wagon stay with units for move. 102nd Bde. move to STEENBECQUE Area. 101st Bde. Repair Lines - also R.A. Group. Lorries deliver direct to 152nd Bde. any to distance. 103rd Bde. move to RENESCURE Area.	
	18th		Tail of Horses of No: 2 Coy: bolted at Dump. 1 Horse shot - no blame attached to anyone. A similar accident occurs to Horses & Wagon	

"ORIGINAL"

Army Form C. 2118.

Instructions regarding War Diaries and Intelligence Summaries are contained in F. S. Regs., Part II. and the Staff Manual respectively. Title pages will be prepared in manuscript.

WAR DIARY
or
INTELLIGENCE SUMMARY.
(Erase heading not required.)

Place	Date	Hour	Summary of Events and Information	Remarks and references to Appendices
FLETRE	18th Feb.		1/16th Royal Scots. Arrange for march for supplies	
ROMBLY	19th		Train H.Q. move to ROMBLY. Found no Billets arranged, so made our own arrangements quite satisfactorily.	
			101st Bde. move to HAZEBROUCK	
			102nd " " ST HILAIRE	
			103rd " " BOESEGHEM	
			R.A. " " STEENBECQUE	
	26th		101st Bde. to ST HILAIRE	
			102 " " DIEVAL	
			103 " " WESTERHEM	
			R.A. " " LAMBRES. Railhead for 102nd Bde. LILLERS - Remainder as Before.	
FREVILLER	27th		Train H.Q. move to CHELERS. its accommodation available to have for 1 night to FREVILLERS.	
			101st Bde. & LA THEOULOYE	
			102nd " " CHELERS	
			103rd " " BORBQ	
			R.A. " " FLORINGHEM	
			D.S.C. " " VALHOUN. Railhead LILLERS for all.	

"ORIGINAL"

Army Form C. 2118.

WAR DIARY
or
INTELLIGENCE SUMMARY.
(Erase heading not required.)

Instructions regarding War Diaries and Intelligence Summaries are contained in F. S. Regs., Part II. and the Staff Manual respectively. Title pages will be prepared in manuscript.

Place	Date	Hour	Summary of Events and Information	Remarks and references to Appendices
	Feb 1917			
CHELERS	22nd		Train H.Qrs moved to CHELERS. 1 N.C.O. & 11 men despatched to THÉROUANNE to fetch 11 limbers & 22 Horses for Infantry Battn. Visited D.D.S. & T. 3rd Army at ST POL. No: 1 Coy Train at NOYELLES No: 2 " " LA THÉOULOYE No: 3 " " LA TIRLET. No: 4 " " ORLANCOURT. Railhead for 102nd Bde ST POL. Remainder LILLERS.	
	23rd		No: 3 Coy; Train to ESCOIVRES. } with their Brigades. No: 4 " " BETHONSART. } Railhead ST POL. Retiring in Group Areas. Tree Dumps established at DIÉVAL – CHELERS – ESCOIVRES.	
	24th		Limbers & Horses arrive – Billet them in CHELERS.	
	25th		Remounts inspected by V.O. and Turn-outs visited & units. Railhead BRYAS. 101st Bde drawn by H.T. & remain loaded over-night.	

T2134. Wt. W708—776. 500000. 4/15. Sir J. C. & S.

"ORIGINAL"

Army Form C. 2118.

WAR DIARY
or
INTELLIGENCE SUMMARY.
(Erase heading not required.)

Instructions regarding War Diaries and Intelligence Summaries are contained in F. S. Regs., Part II. and the Staff Manual respectively. Title pages will be prepared in manuscript.

Place	Date	Hour	Summary of Events and Information	Remarks and references to Appendices
CHELERS	Feb. 1917 26th			
	27th		Arrangements made to cut wood in forest & deliver to Dumps. Railhead AUBIGNY for 102nd & 108th Bde. O.C. T.S.C. agrees to supply 102nd Bde with wood from HABARCQ forest. S.S.O. arranges to supply remainder from CARNOYE. 80 tons of coal arrive in the middle of the night ex LIGNY. All cleared by early morning.	
	28th		All loading to be by M.T. from tomorrow. Groups drawing from BRYAS will load in evening for next day's issue, but as train arrives early at AUBIGNY, will load there in the morning & issue in the afternoon. Therefore 1 day's supplies for 102nd & 103rd Bdes must be kept in R.S.C	

A J Alexander Lt. Col.
O. 34th Div. Train

86DT-861-A — SECRET

H.Q.
34th Division G.

I beg to forward herewith, War Diary Volume No 15 covering the period 1st to 31st March 1917.

A.W. Alexander

Lieut Colonel COMMANDING
84th DIVISIONAL TRAIN,
ARMY SERVICE CORPS.

5-4-17.

WAR DIARY
or
INTELLIGENCE SUMMARY.

Army Form C. 2118.

34 D Train
JC/15

Place	Date	Hour	Summary of Events and Information	Remarks and references to Appendices
CHELERS	March 1917			
	1st		Refitting by Horse Transport commenced for whole Train.	
	2nd		No: 1 Coy. move to LE TIRLET.	
	3rd		Visited new site for Train Camp near "X" Huts and Planned it out.	
	4th		Submitted Indents for material for Ration Dumps. Bus Refilling Point	
	5th		with on main ARRAS ROAD. East of HAUTEAVESNES.	
	6th		Coal Train arrived at LIGNY late at night. With 70 Tons for no. 1 Corps. Detail lorries to remove this to sites indicated by I.S.O.	
			Adjust Personnel etc between Companies to comply with new Establishment.	
	8th		Nos: 2 & 4 Coys: move to new Camp tomorrow. Arranged for Tentage for their accommodation.	
	9th		Issue of Steel Helmets (Obligatory in this Army) from D.A.D.O.S. completed. Nos: 2 & 4 Coys: to new Camp. Extra Blankets issued to their men.	
			No: 3 Coy from ESCOIVRES HUTS to LA THIEULOYE.	
	11th		Authority received to Draw 11 NISSEN HUTS for Camp.	
	12th		Ordered to find an Officer to draw Coal from BRUAY for Corps Hrs. Allotment about 30 Tons for us.	

WAR DIARY or INTELLIGENCE SUMMARY

Army Form C. 2118.

Place	Date	Hour	Summary of Events and Information	Remarks and references to Appendices
	March 1917			
CHELERS	13. P		Have again to find Officer Coal from BRUAY. Erection of Huts in Camp commenced. C.R.E. tends 4 Sappers to assist.	
	15. P		Arranged with A.A. and Q.M.G. for a site for forward Ration Dump in case of an advance. Inspected this site and found it suitable.	
	16. P		No: 1 Coy. moves to New Camp.	
	17. P		No: 3 Coy: from LA THIEULOYE to LE TIRLET. R.A. Refilling Point moved to E.2.3.c	
CAMP E. 18th 29.B.4.6.			Train HdQrs move to New Camp. 102nd Bde Refil from TINQUES by Horse Transport — Refilling S.of CHELERS. Remands to Lorry from TINQUES.	
	20. P		Men received Mufti from TINQUES by Horse Transport from 22nd hote. This means 18 miles for the Horses but it cannot be helped owing to heavy demands on Mechanical Transport. Reft Transport to draw from R.P.	
	21st		No: 2 Coy: to Camp. + No: 4. to LE TIRLET.	
	22nd		New System of Refilling commences. Able to arrange for lorries to draw for 1 Brigade — which relieves Horses a little.	

WAR DIARY or INTELLIGENCE SUMMARY

Army Form C. 2118.

Place	Date	Hour	Summary of Events and Information	Remarks and references to Appendices
	March 1917			
CAMP E.29 B.4.6.	22nd		13 hundred Mules & Personnel attached for duty.	
		2000	Petrol Tins sent to Train for washing & distribution.	
	23rd		Petrol Tins washed. Ordered to hand in 2 Store Tents, 1 Marquee & 6 Bell Tents. As reorganised Infantry in Reserve, Mr Matross are recommended to a minimum & we must improvise Racks for Tarpaulins & Sacks.	
	24th		Refilling Point for Divl. Troops altered to E.14.D.6.0.	
	25th		No. 2 men to ABBEVILLE for 6 Renaults.	
			6 Capts. & 9 men sent to Forward Ration Dump & send-off & parts.	
CAMP E.21.B.4.b.	26th		Iron Rations.	
	29th		No: 1 Coy: 17th Divl: Train attached.	
			Change of Refilling System. Units load at Refuse Dump in Train Camp – Train Wagons load at TINQUES Park loaded Outside their Refilling Points for Refilling next morning. Regt: transport will have supplies thence & our wagons proceed to TINQUES Road.	

A.M.Alexander Lt: Col:
O: C: 34th Divl: Train

WD 196. SECRET

H.Q.,
34th DIVISION G

I beg to forward herewith War Diary covering the period 1st to 30th April 1917 Volume No 16.

A W Alexander
Lieut Colonel
comdg 34th Div Train

3-5-17

WAR DIARY or INTELLIGENCE SUMMARY

Army Form C. 2118.

34 Div Train Vol 16

Place	Date	Hour	Summary of Events and Information	Remarks and references to Appendices
April 1917.				
Camp E.29.B.4.6.	2nd		12 Limbers to Divl. Bomb Store for Duty. 5 G.S. Wagons to Special Coy. R.E. Lt. Hughlin proceeded to XVIII Corps Troops Supply Column. Lt. Thompson appointed S.O. Divl. Troops.	
	3rd		3 HD Horses died from exposure during heavy snow storm. Lt. Brauenden appointed Assistant Divl. Train Officer in forward Area. Petrol Tins for water issued to R.A.	
	4th		Railhead changed to AUBIGNY. 10 Extra Mules Cali dung from Railhead. No. 4 Coy arrived in Camp from Back Area. Erected camp (Mens. Hut.) for S.A.D.O.S. Supplying Kits dumped in Camp for Convoys to Baggage Store TINQUES. 700 2 Gallon & 250 4 gallon Petrol Tins received for washing & mine.	
	5th		Weather improved slightly – some sun. Wagons take Kits to TINQUES & return with Straw from FREVILLERS. Party sent to BOULOGNE for Reinforcements.	
	6th		Continued return of Kits. 103rd Bar Dump at ROELINCOURT blown up replaced.	

WAR DIARY or INTELLIGENCE SUMMARY.

Army Form C. 2118.

Place	Date	Hour	Summary of Events and Information	Remarks and references to Appendices
Camp E.29.	10.4.6		Limbers returned to unit. 2 p. We proceeded at kits to TINCQUES.	
	8th			
	9th		ZERO Day. Visited Bavre HQrs. Snow recommenced.	
	10th		2 water carts sent to each Bde. Removed (18 H.D. arrive) spent with Adjutant up BAILLEUL Road. Most original scheme to see if road was passable for transport. Concurred it was so. With Col Harris Light horse. Whoops Road was in very bad condition. 28 loads gravel to TINCQUES.	
	11th		Visited Corps HQrs with M.A. + O.M.G. to discuss refilling arrangements.	
	12th		Capt. Hutchison took 3 G.S. wagons + 5 limbers to Salvage for temporary duty. Mr. Langholm appointed Dist. Cleaning Officer. Major SHEEBEARE arrived from 17th Div. Temp. Relief over duties of S.S.O.	
	13th		Orders received for next fortnight.	
	14th		Nos. 2, 3 + 4 Coys. move to AVERDOINGT – MONCHY BRETON + CHELERS. Arranged move of troops. Also to troops from the Trenches at DEAD MAN'S CORNER. Issue complete at 12.45 pm.	

WAR DIARY or INTELLIGENCE SUMMARY

Army Form C. 2118

Place	Date	Hour	Summary of Events and Information	Remarks and references to Appendices
CHELERS	15th April 1917		Train H.Qrs moved to CHELERS. Refilling for Div. less Artillery on main ARRAS – ST POL Road ½ mile W of TINQUETTE.	
"	16th		No: 4 Coy moved from CHELERS & BAILLEUL – AIX – CORNEILLES. Inspected Companies, who have most of their horses under cover, which will give them an opportunity to pick up lost condition. Orders received to refill M.H.T. tomorrow from TINQUES. Railhead changed from AUBIGNY to TINQUES. R.A. Railhead. AGNEZ.	
"	17th			
"	20th		Sent wagon to Chelers Derelict Petrol Dump as a precaution for want of supplies in forward area. Major Stidwell leaves tonight to join 18th Reserve Park.	
LARESSET	21st		Railhead changed to AGNEZ. Train H.Qrs Nos: 2, 3 & 4 Coys' move to LARESSET.	
"	22nd		Refilling main ARRAS – ST POL Road ¼ mile W of HAUTE AVESNES. Lieut: Smith joined & was posted to No: 3 Coy; Lieut: MacDonald appointed Town Major – LARESSET.	
"	23rd		Refilling ¼ mile W of Y. Huts. ARRAS – ST POL Road	
"	25th		Lieut: Blackburne & 3 O.R. taken over South Kitchen in forward area. S.S.O – took me advanced Ration Dump from 51st Division. Railhead the ARRAS from tomorrow. Installed ARRAS Station (broad & branch line GRANDE PLACE).	
"	26th		arrangements. Refilling here on branch line GRANDE PLACE.	

WAR DIARY or INTELLIGENCE SUMMARY

Army Form C. 2118

(Erase heading not required.)

Place	Date	Hour	Summary of Events and Information	Remarks and references to Appendices
LARESSET	29 April 1917.		Railhead changed to ARRAS. Refilling at 9, 14, a (59 B.) near S.P. CATHERINE. Orders for Nos: 2 & 4 Coy: to move tomorrow.	
	30 "			

A.J. Alexander Lt. Col:
O.C. 34th Divl: Train

Army Form C. 2118

WAR DIARY
or
INTELLIGENCE SUMMARY

3 4 D Train

May 17

(Erase heading not required.)

Instructions regarding War Diaries and Intelligence Summaries are contained in F.S. Regs., Part II. and the Staff Manual respectively. Title Pages will be prepared in manuscript.

Place	Date	Hour	Summary of Events and Information	Remarks and references to Appendices
LARESSET	1st May 1917.		101st & 103rd Bdes Refill in Camp – R.A. & 102nd Bde as usual. M.T. in relation for whole Division.	
LE CAUROY	2nd		No: 2 Coy. horses to SUS ST LEGER – No: 4 to RULLECOURT. Moved Train H.Q.rs to LE CAUROY. No: 3 Coy. to BARLY. Lorries dump for Re-filling in new areas.	
– " –	3rd		Railhead SAULTY.	
– " –	6a.		No: 2 Coy. to BOUQUEMAISON.	
BERNAVILLE	7a.		T.H.Q. to BERNAVILLE. No: 2 Coy. to EPECAMPS. No: 3 to SUS ST LEGER – No: 4 to BOUQUEMAISON.	
– " –	8a.		Lt COL: ALEXANDER to Paris on leave. MAJ: TWEEDY takes over temporary command of the Train. No: 3 Coy: to BOUQUEMAISON – No: 4 Coy: to CANAPLES. Railhead CANDAS.	
– " –	9a.		Horse Transport draws from Railhead for 101st & 103rd Bdes No: 3 Coy to FIENVILLERS.	
– " –	11a.		New A.A. & Q.M.G. (Lt: Col: TYLER) visits Railhead, Dumps & 1st Line Transport.	
– " –	12a.		Lt: Col: ALEXANDER returns from leave.	
– " –	– " –		20 H.P. Remounts arrive & are distributed. A very good lot.	
– " –	14a.		A.D.V.S. inspects Train Horses. He considers we have picked up well except No: 3 Coy. Instructions given for continual grazing & other improvements.	
– " –	16a.		G.O.C. Division inspects Train Companies & is very pleased with Turn-Out.	

1875 Wt. W593/826 1,000,000 4/15 J.B.C. & A. A.D.S.S./Forms/C. 2118.

Army Form C. 2118

WAR DIARY
or
INTELLIGENCE SUMMARY
(Erase heading not required.)

Instructions regarding War Diaries and Intelligence Summaries are contained in F. S. Regs., Part II. and the Staff Manual respectively. Title Pages will be prepared in manuscript.

Place	Date	Hour	Summary of Events and Information	Remarks and references to Appendices
	May: 1917			
BERNAVILLE	14th			
	18th		2/Lieut: Hardwicke returns to the Train from Hospital.	
	22nd		G.O.C. Division sends special congratulatory order on his inspection for Pettishor. Application made for return of Cor. temporarily detached to A.P.O. since January. Experiments made with several devices for carrying water on limbers in Pilot Train. Selected one, a wooden one, a wooden tank on Amb: of Rear limber.	
	24th		Arrangements made to take over camp of 17th Divisional Train on our return to Forward Area.	
	25th		Draw 3 Remounts (Riders) - Chest show the same great improvement in quality found in recent H.D. Remounts.	
	26th		101st & 103rd Brigade Refill since as a preliminary to move.	
	27th		101st & 103rd Brigades move to SAULTY and LEHALERIE. Inspected on route & found March discipline very good. Horses improved condition enabled them to bear long march (22 miles) well. 102nd Bde Refill since	
	28th		No: 3 Coy. to COUTRELLE.	
	29th			
	30th		T.H.Q. move to new Camp. (G.14 a 51.6) . No: 3 Coy: arrive in Camp.	
Camp (G.14.a 51.6)	31st		No: 2 Coy: arrive Railhead ARRAS - drawing by H.T.	

AW Alexander Lt: Col:
O.C: 34th Divisional Train.

WAR DIARY or INTELLIGENCE SUMMARY

Army Form C. 2118

34 Div.ⁿˡ Train WO/95/2462

Place	Date	Hour	Summary of Events and Information	Remarks and references to Appendices
Camp G.14.a.5,7 B.	1ˢᵗ June 1917	—	Refilling 8.30 am. Railhead 11 am.	
	2ⁿᵈ	—	4 wagons for R.E. Salipré in forward area nightly.	
	4ᵗʰ	—	Lieut: Aiken promoted Captain. St Price & 2 Horses killed by shell fire in R.E. Salipré	
	6ᵗʰ	—	Begin construction of Ration Dumps at Refilling Point. Information received	
			that 111ᵗʰ Army H.Q.rs move to ALBERT.	
	7ᵗʰ	—	Comᵈ of 2 giving wagons of H.P. Horse from R.A. H.Q. G.P.O lines on 1ˢᵗ instant.	
			R.E. Salipré cancelled.	
	8ᵗʰ	—	Sergt: Faulkner received M.S. Medal in "Honours" list.	
	9ᵗʰ	—	Inspected all companies in detail at Refilling Point — Exceptionally good	
			turn-out — wonderful improvement in condition of horses & harness.	
	12ᵗʰ	—	Inspected R.A. Baggage wagons. Condition indifferent — made arrangements	
			for them to be splenetically overhauled	
	15ᵗʰ	—	Warning order for Division to move to Rest Area -18ᵗʰ approximately.	
			Lieut: Col. ALEXANDER proceeds on leave — Major TWEEDY takes over	
			Command of Train	
	16ᵗʰ	—	A.A. & Q.M.G. inspects supply wagons at Refilling Point.	
	17ᵗʰ	—	293 Bde R.F.A. Crossed off strength provision.	

Army Form C. 2118

WAR DIARY
or
INTELLIGENCE SUMMARY

ORIGINAL

(Erase heading not required.)

Instructions regarding War Diaries and Intelligence Summaries are contained in F.S. Regs., Part II. and the Staff Manual respectively. Title Pages will be prepared in manuscript.

Place	Date	Hour	Summary of Events and Information	Remarks and references to Appendices
Camp G.14.a.	18th		H.Q: section. No: 2 Co: move to MONCHEAUX. Supply wagons drawn from ARRAS at 9 am v follow.	
"	19th		Refilling for 1st & 2nd Bde by Motor Transport 10 am. C.Q.M.S. hand reconnoitred for commanders in A.S.C.	
"	20th		No: 2 Coy: drawn by M.T. & delivers supplies in new area	
"	21st		No: 3 Coy: move to BUNEVILLE. Supply section Drs from ARRAS at 9 am v follow.	
"	23rd		No: 4 Coy: move to MAIZIERES. Train M.D. G/3 to HERMAVILLE	
			All companies noted in new area. Arrangements satisfactory, except for water. Water lorries arranged for to deliver daily to 3 & 4 Coy: also lorries to take forage to H.Q: 1 Coy: in forward area trines weekly.	
"	25th		Letter received from G.H.Q.1R. say that all Offrs: of Arti: Trans: under 30 will be gradually withdrawn v transferred to Infantry	
			A.A. v Q.M.G. inspects 3 & 4 Coy:	
"	26th		Lieut: Col: Alexander returns from leave v takes over command of Train. A.D.V.S. inspects Horses of R8th Companies v concludes them in every satisfactory condition.	
"	27th		Major Shepherd (S.S.O.) goes on leave. Major Tready takes over his duties.	

A.S.Alexander Lieut: Col:
Comdg. 34th Divisional Train

SECRET

34DT 567

H.Q.
34th Division G.S.

I beg to forward
herewith War Diary volume
No 13 covering the period
1st to 31st July 1918.

AW Alexander
Lieut Colonel
Comdg 34th Division Train
A.S.C

8-8-18

Army Form C. 2118

Nov 19

WAR DIARY
or
INTELLIGENCE SUMMARY
(Erase heading not required.)

Instructions regarding War Diaries and Intelligence Summaries are contained in F.S. Regs., Part II. and the Staff Manual respectively. Title Pages will be prepared in manuscript.

Place	Date	Hour	Summary of Events and Information	Remarks and references to Appendices
	July 1917			
HERMAVILLE	1st		Division to move on 4th, 5th, & 6th.	
"	3rd		Arrangements made for all Officers under 30 to be medically examined as to fitness for transfer to Infantry.	
"	4th		101st & 102nd Bde Refill Unit in preparation for move.	
"	4th		No. 1 Coy. move with R.A. to VII- Corps Area. S.S.O. sent for to H.Q. Cav. Corps & arranges Bremen in new area. No. 2 & 3 Coys entrain at LIGNY - No. 4 at TINCQUES. All arrangements work very smoothly.	
"	6th		Train H.Q. Q.M. move to PÉRONNE.	
PÉRONNE	9th		ROISEL - 1 & 4 near PÉRONNE. Lt-Adjt. Miller takes over duties of Area Commandant ROISEL temporarily.	
"			No: 1 & 4 Coys: move to Camp near ROISEL. Railhead ROISEL.	
ROISEL	10th		Train H.Q. move to ROISEL. IIIrd Corps take over area, including 84 F.D.S.	
"	11th		Major Shelton returns from leave & takes over duties of S.S.S.	
"	12th		All Companies drawn from Railhead by Horse Transport. relinquishes Area Commandant duties.	
"	13th		13. I.F.D. Horse S.L.P. Remounts distributed.	
"	15th		All Stores in Huts & Wheels to be removed. This has never been & any use to the Train. Who hitherto have had no leaves.	

WAR DIARY
or
INTELLIGENCE SUMMARY.
(Erase heading not required.)

Army Form C. 2118.

Place	Date	Hour	Summary of Events and Information	Remarks and references to Appendices
ROISEL	18th		A.A. & Q.M.G. inspected Refilling Points & Camps. He considered them remarkably good.	
"	20th		Capt: Mayne appointed member of Committee for Divisional Horse Show.	
"	22nd		A long distance gun put 28 shells near our Camps & Refilling Points. All horses were removed expeditiously & no harm was done.	
"	23rd		No: 2 (br): directed to construct Experimental Manure Sump.	Wagon Track along Slope. Each side thrown some manure daily.
"	26th		Iron Shelters for Refilling Points drawn from Corps. An excellent Pattern. Bolted together and easily moved.	
"	30th		Submitted Scheme for Wire Refilling Points. To be 10yds off ROISEL-NORESCOURT Road. Metalled Roadways the width round each leading to & from the Road.	
"	31st		2/Lt Hardwicke ordered to proceed at once to England, under instructions for transferring Tempr Officers to Infantry.	

A. S Alexander Lt: Col:
OC. 34 Divl: Train.

34DT 812

SECRET

H.Q.
34th Division G.S.

I beg to forward herewith "War Diary" volume No 20 covering the period 1st to 31st August 1917.

A W Alexander
Lieut Colonel
Comdg 34th DIVISIONAL TRAIN,
ARMY SERVICE CORPS.

8-9-17

WAR DIARY or INTELLIGENCE SUMMARY

Army Form C. 2118.

"ORIGINAL" 34 D Train

Place	Date	Hour	Summary of Events and Information	Remarks and references to Appendices
ROISEL	1917 1st August		2/Lieut: Hardwicke proceeded to 2nd Infantry School, Belford.	
"	3rd		Refilling Point changed to MONTIGNY FARM. Shelter supplies are conveyed by Decauville Railway. 1st line Transport draws from Dump.	
"	4th		2/Lieut: Grove reported for duty. Only 15 wagons to be arrived in yard at a time at Refilling Point.	
"	8th		Inspection of Horses under new scheme by which 12 Riders are to be replaced by Bicycles. D.D.S.T. 3rd Army (Col. Swoboda) accompanied by D.D.V.S. Inspected the Train. D.D.S.T. very pleased with the Train & commented particularly on the Horses.	
"	11th		Lieut. & Adjt. MILLER to England on leave. 2/Lt: BRISENDEN takes over as Adjutant. 20 men sent to VERMAND to relieve Haymaking Party temporarily.	
"	12th		20 horses sent to VERMAND to graze - relieve pressure of work in train due to so many men being away.	
"	13th		Divisional Horse Show. Train won 8 prizes. ROISEL again shelled by Long Distance Gun. R.S.O. being wrecked to the Casualties & damage.	
"	14th		Capt: CROSBY. M.C. reported for duty. Conference with C.R.E at Refilling Point with reference to building up Platforms into Sleepers. C.R.E. promised to get this done. 2/Lt: HALL reported for duty.	

Army Form C. 2118.

ORIGINAL

WAR DIARY
or
INTELLIGENCE SUMMARY.
(Erase heading not required.)

Instructions regarding War Diaries and Intelligence Summaries are contained in F.S. Regs., Part II. and the Staff Manual respectively. Title pages will be prepared in manuscript.

Place	Date	Hour	Summary of Events and Information	Remarks and references to Appendices
ROISEL	14th		Divisional Transportation Officer appointed to consolidate all Requisitions for transport.	
"	16th		Divisional Commander given authority for heit's & Adj: MILLER to arrange leaves of Reont as by Capt:	
"	17th		Horses returned from VERMAND as Officer i/c Haymakers cannot spare men to look after them.	
"	23rd		Visited proposed new Brigade Refilling Points into A.A. & Q.M.G. Points were selected to which Decauville Railway will eventually deliver Supplies, the object being to keep lorries off the Roads as much as possible.	
"	24th		Capt & Adj: MILLER returned from leave.	
"	25th		Authority received to have 50 Boys of Notting under training Scheme.	
"	26th		All Supply Clerks medically inspected with a view to transfer to Infantry.	
"	31st		Adj: & Adj: MILLER to proceed to 2nd Infantry School. Sept: New Refilling Point for 157 Bde & 104 D.A. nr VERMAND.	A.S. Alexander Lt Col CRE 34th Divl Train

2333 Wt. W544/1454 700,000 5/15 D. D. & L. A.D.S.S./Forms/C. 2118.

3ADT/18   Secret

H.Q.
34th Division C.S.

I beg to forward herewith
"War Diary" Volume No 21 covering
the period 1st to 30th September 1917

AW Alexander
Lieut Colonel
Cmdg 34th DIVISIONAL TRAIN,
ARMY SERVICE CORPS.

12-10-17

Army Form C. 2118.

"Original"
3 4 D Train
Vol 21

WAR DIARY
or
INTELLIGENCE SUMMARY.
(Erase heading not required.)

Instructions regarding War Diaries and Intelligence Summaries are contained in F. S. Regs., Part II. and the Staff Manual respectively. Title pages will be prepared in manuscript.

Place	Date	Hour	Summary of Events and Information	Remarks and references to Appendices
	September 1917			
ROISEL	1st September		Parade of Horses for inspection by Committee from Board of Agriculture with a view to selection for breeding purposes.	
"	2nd		Lieut: Mitchell reported to Train H.Q.rs as a/Adjutant to replace t/Capt: Miller who proceeded to England for Infantry Training.	
"	8th		Admitted for medical required. complete States. Lieut. Mitchell appointed Adjutant	
"	11.		Patrol Officers detailed daily to supervise work on roads & to visit to the wants of alarms of Transport. III rd Corps Horse parade inspected Train Horses.	
"	12th		6. P.B. Clerks report from Base.	
"	15.		Horses k/e dipped at BEAUMETZ as Preventive to Skin Disease.	
"	17.		Divisional Commander inspected lines. Expressed satisfaction. Inspected No 1 Coy.	
"	18th		Should have a Dining Room.	
"	26 th		Beds for Admin. Hut – in No:1 Coy' Lines drawn. Lieut.Col: Alexander proceeds on leave. Major Tweedy taken over command of Train.	
"	27th		No: 2 Coy: moves to BAPAUME – first stage of move. No: 3 Coy to BAPAUME – No 2 to BIENVILLERS – Lt Harrison & Promoten to Infantry School.	
"	28th		No: 4 Coy to BAPAUME – No: 3 to BAILLEULVAL.	

Army Form C. 2118.

"Original"

WAR DIARY
or
INTELLIGENCE SUMMARY.
(Erase heading not required.)

Place	Date	Hour	Summary of Events and Information	Remarks and references to Appendices
ROISEL	29th Sept.		No. 4 Coy to HENDECOURT. Train H.Qrs to BAISEUX - R.A. Group (with No.1 Coy) to PERONNE - DOINGT Area.	
BAISEUX	30th		"M": Forlow joined - was posted to No. 4 Coy. "M": Groves transferred to No. 3.	

A.S.Alexander Lt. Col.
It. 30th Divisional Train.

34 DT 913   Secret

H.Q.
34th Division C.

I beg to forward herewith
War Diary Volume No 22 covering
the period 1st to 31st October 1917.

W.J. Alexander
Lieut Colonel
Comdg 34th DIVISIONAL TRAIN
ARMY SERVICE CORPS

7.11.17

WAR DIARY or INTELLIGENCE SUMMARY

Army Form C. 2118.

34 D Train   Vol 22

Places	Date	Hour	Summary of Events and Information	Remarks and references to Appendices
BOISEUX	October 1917			
	2nd Oct		No. 3 Coy: Given motor lorry for water. Honours list submitted	
	5th		15 Surplus Riders sent to ALBERT. Reinf. Dept.	
	7th		No. 2 Coy: leave by Train for PROVEN. 9 am. No. 4 at 12 noon. T.H.Q. move to PROVEN.	
PROVEN	8th		No. 3 Coy: move to PROVEN	
	9th		No. 1 Coy: arrive from PERONNE.	
	11th		No. 4 Coy: move to A.24.b.80. Sheet 28 after second Refilling	
	12th		No. 3 Coy: move to new Camp.	
	13th		Railhead – INTERNATIONAL CORNER	
	14th		No. 2 Coy + T.H.Q. to new camp.	
A.24.b.80	18th		Nos: 2, 3 + 4 Coys: move to A.18.b.55. All Horses in open except No. 2 Personnel in Tents. Train N.Q.: Train N.Q. moves to A.18.b.5.	
	20th		19.S.S. Major attached to Depot B2 at ACHEKE. Enemy Aircraft dropped several Bombs near Train Camp. One falling into Road about 6.30 pm. Killed 1 man + 16 Horses + injured 3 men + 15 Horses. All No. 4 Coy.	
	23rd		1, 3 + 4 Coys: move to PROVEN. No. 1 Coy: to A.2.b.9.1.	
	24th		T.H.Q. to PROVEN. 32 H.B. Remounts arrive to replace casualties. ACHIET.	
	28th		No. 4 Coy: leave by Train for BOISLEUX. Bt. Train + Adj. also leave for BOISLEUX	

WAR DIARY
or
INTELLIGENCE SUMMARY.

(Erase heading not required.)

Army Form C. 2118.

Place	Date	Hour	Summary of Events and Information	Remarks and references to Appendices
ACHIET.	29	-	No. 2 Coy: - T.H.Q. Move by Train to ACHIET LE PETIT. No. 3 Coy: to BOISLEUX. No. 1 Coy: move from ACHIET to BOISLEUX.	
"	31st	-		

A.W. Alexander Lt. Col.
O/i 34th Div Sup Train

ACHIET

SECRET

> 34th DIV. TRAIN, A.S.C.
> 1 3 DEC. 1917
> No. D.T. 55

H.Q.
34th Div. A.S.C.

I beg to forward herewith War Diary Volume N° 218 covering the period 1st – 30th Nov 1917.

A.W. Alexander
Lieut Col
Cdg 34th DIVISIONAL TRAIN,
ARMY SERVICE CORPS.

13th Dec 1917

"ORIGINAL"

Army Form C. 2118.

WAR DIARY
or
INTELLIGENCE SUMMARY. 34 D Train

(Erase heading not required.)

Vol 23

Instructions regarding War Diaries and Intelligence Summaries are contained in F.S. Regs., Part II, and the Staff Manual respectively. Title pages will be prepared in manuscript.

Place	Date	Hour	Summary of Events and Information	Remarks and references to Appendices
ACHIET-LE-PETIT	1st November 1917		Supplies drawn in Brun from Decauville Railway.	
BOISLEUX-AU-MONT	2nd		Train H.Qrs moves to BOISLEUX-AU-MONT. Supplies drawn by Horse Transport. Train Camp exceedingly muddy. Div: Troops Supply drawn by Decauville. Food in every way.	
"	7th		S.S.O. (Major Shebbeare) goes on leave. Duties taken on by Capt: Jack.	
"	9th		No: 1. Coy: (with Div: Artillery) arrives at BOISLEUX. Their future Camp being still occupied by No: 4 Coy. 62nd Train. Meanwhile they are accommodated temporarily in 8th Coy: Camps.	
"	16th		Div: Troops Southampton being Railhead Refilling.	
"	16th		17 L.D. Horses collected & placed on Lines of No: 4 Coy: pending same as Remounts.	
"	23rd		Major Shebbeare returns from leave.	
"	24th		Traffic Control Officer (O.C. 5 Companies Jr Inst) appointed Traffic at Railhead.	
"	28th		Adj: (Capt: Pritchett) goes on leave. Lieut: Smith to be A/Adj. 2/Lt. Roche in Temporary Command No: 3 Co: vice Lieut: Smith	

A.J. Allenwold Lt. Col.
O.C. 34th D.T. Train

WAR DIARY
or
INTELLIGENCE SUMMARY.

(Erase heading not required.)

Army Form C. 2118.

Place	Date	Hour	Summary of Events and Information	Remarks and references to Appendices
BOISLEUX- AU-MONT.	December 1917.			
	2nd		Lieut: BARTON appointed Divl: Claims Officer vice Lt: LAUGHTON.	
"	6th		Capt: JACK Transferred to Infantry School - Berford.	
"	9th		2/Lt: LESLIE posted to Command No: 2 Coy.	
"	10th		A.O.C: Division inspected 3 & 4 Companies. Inspection very complete. Result quite satisfactory.	
"	12th		Several Bombs dropped by Enemy Aircraft near Train Camp. No damage. Visited D.D. S.T. III rd Army with S.S.O.	
"	14th		G.O.C. inspected 1 & 2 Companies and was quite satisfied. Adjutant (Capt: Michan) returned from leave. Shaw Precautions put into force.	
"	25th		new Refilling Point opened at BOYELLES.	
"	27th		Capts: ADKIN & MILLIGAN Transferred to Infantry School - Berford.	
"	28th		mentioned in Sir Douglas HAIG'S Despatches. Major SKERBEARE - T/Lieut- (now Capt.) H.G.V. MILLER - T/2/Lt- (now Lt) C.C. BRISSENDEN - S.S.M. REPTON.	
"	29th		S: THURWELL (No: 4 Coy) awarded Card of Honour by G.O.C. for Courageous Conduct near ELVERDINGHE when Train Camp was bombed by E.A.	

aus Alexander Lt. Col.
O.C. 34 Divl Train

34th DIV. TRAIN, A.S.C.

5 - FEB 1918

No. DT/118

H.Q.
34th Division G.

Beg to forward herewith
War Diary volume No. 215 covering
the period 1st to 31st January 1918.

A W Allen
Lieut Col
34th DIVISIONAL TRAIN
ARMY SERVICE CORPS

5.2.18

34th Div. Train

Army Form C. 2118.

WAR DIARY
or
INTELLIGENCE SUMMARY.
(Erase heading not required.)

Place	Date	Hour	Summary of Events and Information	Remarks and references to Appendices
BOISLEUX ST MARC	January 1918			
"	5th		Major Tinecoth takes over Command of Train during absence & Paris of Lt. Col. Alexander.	
"	7th		A.A. & Q.M.G. inspects new Draft Cops on hafn. Wheeled vehicles Horse outfits	
"	8th		13 Remounts Collected from BAPAUME	
"	10th		Lt. Col. Alexander returns from leave.	
"	13th		Inspection of stable Carts by I.O.S.	
"			Major Massey - Westropp attached to Train for Instruction for 3 days. Passed 18/1/18.	
"	19th		Coy. for Transport Work 2 days. S.S.O. 2 days. T.H.Q. Ideas.	
"	27th		All Remits Inspected by Brig. M.Forster Elphinstone "A" V.B.	
"			Capt. Magire transferred to M.T. School - FISHER.	
BERRY-ST-RICHTRUDE	29th		T.H.Q. moves to T.H.Q. 3rd Division at BOICY ST RICHTRUDE.	

A.W. Alexander Lt.-Col.
Lt. 34th Divisional Train

Army Form C. 2118.

WAR DIARY
or
INTELLIGENCE SUMMARY.
(Erase heading not required.)

34 D Train JDC 2 Corps

Instructions regarding War Diaries and Intelligence Summaries are contained in F.S. Regs. Part II. and the Staff Manual respectively. Title pages will be prepared in manuscript.

Place	Date	Hour	Summary of Events and Information	Remarks and references to Appendices
BOIRY-ST-RICTRUDE	February 1918.			
	6th	-	LIEUT COL: ALEXANDER on leave. 2/LT. R. SIMPSON TWEEDY taken over Command of Train.	
	7th	-	2/LIEUT: (CAPT.) MICHELL Supplies Officer on leave. 2/LT. MERRETT assumed Appointment of Adjutant.	
	8th	-	MAJOR R.V.C. YOUNG proceeded to 102nd Field Amb.	
	9th	-	No:4 Coy: proceeded to Rest Area.	
	10th	-	No:2 Coy: to Rest Area.	
			No:1-Coy: No:3 Coy: Train Hd. Qrs. to Rest Area (LE CAUROY)	
BERLENCOURT	11th	-	All settled in Rest area. Billets fair. 15 offs. and horses except No.4 Coys. in Rear.	
	15th	-	Heads/Qrs. MERRETT delivered 15 new lorries to Park 4th of Can: Corps.	
	16th	-	Div. Coys: handed over Nos. 2 & 3 Com: Coys. as at 10 A.M.	
	18th	-	Rich Column new lorries No.1 Company.	
	20th	-	Heads: COL: ALEXANDER Return from leave & assumed Command of Train.	
	21st	-	D.A.C. Commander inspected No:4 Company.	
	22nd	-		
	27th	-	Nos. 2, 3 & 4 Companies moved in to BONNIERES AREA.	
	28th	-	From Hd. Qrs. to BOIRY-ST-RICTRUDE.	

Col: Alexander Lt Col.
O.C. 34th D.T. Train

D.T. 214

SECRET

H.Q.
34th Division C.S.

I beg to forward herewith War Diary Volume No. 27 covering the period 1st–31st March 1918. The delay in rendering same is regretted but is quite unavoidable owing to the Unit being continuously on the move recently and the necessary documents in consequence being inaccessible.

A.W. Alexander
Lieut Colony
O/C 34th Divisional Train
A.S.C.

20-11-18.

Army Form C. 2118.

34 D Train
Vol 27

WAR DIARY or INTELLIGENCE SUMMARY

(Erase heading not required.)

Place	Date	Hour	Summary of Events and Information	Remarks and references to Appendices
BOIRY ST.-RICTRUDE	1st March 1918			
"	3rd		1 N.C.O. ~ 2 H.D. Horses sent to PREVENT for Amiens wagon. 1 N.C.O. ~ 1 Coy returned from REBREUVIETTE.	
"	15th		Warning received that in certain eventualities, Rear Divl. H.Q. may have to be accommodated in Train Camp.	
"	16th		Steps taken to improve Anti-Aircraft Defences in the Camp.	
"	21st		Enemy Attack. Camp heavily shelled. Anti-Aircraft Defences proved efficient service and 1 Horse wounded was the only casualty.	
"	22nd		Visited D.H.Q. in the Sup. Coln at COMMIECOURT and received orders to move the Train at once to DOUCHY-LES-AYETTE. In spite of very heavy traffic this was quickly done & without confusion. Railhead moved to BEAUMETZ. Horses drew supplies at Train Camp – BOIRY. Thence the Supply wagons carried them to DOUCHY.	
DOUCHY-LES-AYETTE	23rd		Orders having been received that Division would move on Relief, to SOUASTRE area, supplies were dumped by lorries at SOUASTRE. R.A. drew by H.T. from BEAUMETZ – a 20 mile march, but unavoidable as sufficient lorries were not available.	
"	24		Move to SOUASTRE Cancelled. The supplies dumped in that Area were consequently packed as the Day in Hand, and H.T. drew from...	

2353 Wt. W2541/1454 700,000 5/15 D.D.&L. A.D.S.S./Form3/C. 2118.

Army Form C. 2118.

WAR DIARY
or
INTELLIGENCE SUMMARY.
(Erase heading not required.)

Instructions regarding War Diaries and Intelligence Summaries are contained in F.S. Regs., Part II. and the Staff Manual respectively. Title pages will be prepared in manuscript.

Place	Date	Hour	Summary of Events and Information	Remarks and references to Appendices
			BEAUMETZ and delivered to Train Camp for immediate issue by M.T. & Artillery	
BASSEUX	25th		Train moved to BASSEUX.	
	26th		Train moved to LE CAUROY. Supplies drawn from Railhead by H.T. for Artillery - Replacing Point LIERCOURT. Lorries picked up supplies left at SOURSTRE and delivered to Replacing Point.	
LE CAUROY			Train moved to AUXI - LE - CHATEAU. Supply wagons marched full - Railhead changed to FREVENT where drew supplies & delivered to R.P. at AUXI - LE - CHATEAU. During the march there were numerous haltings. Came Cars & Cavalry had broken through the line & Train Companies were met in the way & moved to area west of AUXI. A later & stood down before being removed into. Supplies were delivered to Units	
AUXI - LE - CHATEAU	27th		Division ordered to entrain at PETIT HOUVIN & FREVENT. Train to move by March Route to ST. POL area. Railhead AUXI - LE - CHATEAU, whence supplies were drawn by M.T. & delivered to entraining stations. Train H.Q.rs moved to MERVILLE.	
MERVILLE	28th		Train Companies moved to CHOCQUES area. Railhead BRUAY.	
"	29th		Companies arrived at MERVILLE area. Railhead MERVILLE. Train H.Q.r.s.	
LE SART	31st		moved to LE SART. moved to STEENWERCK.	

A W Alexander Lt Col.
OC 24th Div.l. Train

Army Form C. 2118.

WAR DIARY
or
INTELLIGENCE SUMMARY.
(Erase heading not required.)

3rd Div Engineers

Place	Date	Hour	Summary of Events and Information	Remarks and references to Appendices
Commencourt	22/3/18		During night of 22/23 Division moved to Ayette	
Ayette Aitrupes	23/3/18		Whole Division moved from Ayette to Adinfer	
Adinfer Basseux	24/3/18		Division moved from Adinfer to Basseux	
Basseux Liancourt	25/3/18		Division moved from Basseux to Liancourt	
Le Cauroy Auxi-le-Château	26/3/18		Division moved from Liancourt to Auxi-le-Château	
Auxi-le-Château	27/3/18		Orders received to move to Merville	
Merville	28/3/18		Offr closed at Auxi-le-Château 9am opened same hour at Merville	
Merville	29/3/18		Orders received that Division relieving 38th Division at Stenwerk. 53rd engr	
Merville	30/3/18		Visited RyET? ? dth HQ near Erquinghem. Recon Rd. HQ at Erquinghem and left	
Merville Stenwerk	31/3/18		Battle of Pont factory Committee observed Merville at ?b send inchqua at Stenwerk at the commence	

H.Q.
34th Division A.S.

I beg to forward herewith War Diary Vol. No. 28 covering the period 1st to 30th April 1918.

A.V. Alexander
Lieut Colonel
Cdg 84th DIVISIONAL TRAIN,
ARMY SERVICE CORPS

15-5-18

GSO IT
To deal

WAR DIARY or INTELLIGENCE SUMMARY

Army Form C. 2118.

"ORIGINAL" Vol 28

Place	Date	Hour	Summary of Events and Information	Remarks and references to Appendices
	April - 1918			
STEENWERCK	1st April	-	- nil -	
"	2nd	-	Inspected Company Camps. On the whole very poor. No: 2 Coy: by no means so good as the others - made arrangements for improvements	
"	8th	-	No: 1 Coy: arrived	
S. of B-S Road	9th	-	Enemy attacked with great vigour. In consequence of pressure on the Right, our HQ. moved to S. of BAILLEUL - STRAZEELE Road - Train Companies to BLANCHE - MAISON. Had 2 Refilling - 6th Group marching with Supply Section full.	
"	10th	-	Railhead changed to STRAZEELE. Refilling at BLANCHE MAISON. But Troops in MOTTE. Companies moved to OUTERSTEENE. Train HQ. personnel/mule defensive duties on Railway.	
"	11th	-	Refilling BAILLEUL - OUTERSTEENE Road. T. HQ. moved to LE GRAND HAZARD. Train Companies to BORRE.	
LE GRAND HAZARD	12th	-	Railhead EBBLINGHEM. Exchanged No: 1 Coy for corresponding Coy. 38th Divl. Train. Refilled at BORRE except 39th & 34th Divl. Troops (at MORBECQUE). All moved in the evening at short notice to GODWAERSWELDE.	
GODWAERSVELDE	13th	-	Refilled main Squares. Moved into Camps M.W. of Town -	

Army Form C. 2118

WAR DIARY
or
INTELLIGENCE SUMMARY
(Erase heading not required.)

Instructions regarding War Diaries and Intelligence Summaries are contained in F. S. Regs., Part II. and the Staff Manual respectively. Title Pages will be prepared in manuscript.

Place	Date	Hour	Summary of Events and Information	Remarks and references to Appendices
GODWAERSVELDE	14th	—	Railheads – EBBLINGHEM for 38th Divl. Artillery – WIPPENHOEK for remainder.	
"	17th	—	Camp shelled all night – moved to GODWAERSVELDE – STEENWOORDE Road.	
STEENWOORDE	18th	—	T.H.Q. moved to LEEWERKE between Div. H.Q. (at BOESHEEPE)	
LEEWERKE	19th	—	Replied on GODWAERSVELDE – BEAUVORDE Road.	
"	22nd	—	Moved Train to ST JAN TER BIEZEN. Very dirty + insanitary Camp.	
ST JAN TER BIEZEN	24th	—	Camp heavily Bombed – No Casualties.	
"	26th	—	Railhead ZWAARTSHOEK – Very small new Railhead in exposed position.	
"	27th	—	Railhead heavily shelled just after our wagons left. Sixth Road N. of POPERINGH – also shelled.	
"	28th	—	Railhead INTERNATIONAL CORNER. Roads very congested.	
"	29th	—	Railhead ROUSBRUGGE. T.H.Q. + 2 & 3 Corps moved to 28.K.L.D. 9.9. M.4.	
28.K.L.D. 9.9.	30th	—	Loc: OOST CAPEL.	
			Refilling at Train Camp.	

A. S. Allen Lieut. Col.
O.C. 34th Divl. Train.

1875 Wt. W593/826 1,000,000 4/15 J.B.C. & A. A.D.S.S./Forms/C. 2118.

H.Q.
34th Division A.S.

I beg to forward herewith War Diary Volume 29 covering the period 1st–31st May 1918. I regret the delay in forwarding this Diary owing to same having not been circulated.

22-6-1918

Lieut Colonel
34th DIVISIONAL TRAIN,
ARMY SERVICE CORPS

G.S.O. 1st

"ORIGINAL"

34 D Train

Vol 29

Army Form C. 2118

WAR DIARY or INTELLIGENCE SUMMARY

(Erase heading not required.)

Place	Date	Hour	Summary of Events and Information	Remarks and references to Appendices
Camp 28.K.L.8.9.9.	1st May 1918	—	Rifilling Point for No: 4 Co: moved to OOST CAPEL.	
"	2nd	—	No: 4 Coy: moved to Train Camp.	
"	8th	—	No: 2 Coy: moved to HOUTKERQUE.	
"	12th	—	Train Hd Qrs: Nos: 2 & 3 Coys: moved to RUBROUK — No: 4 Coy En route for LUMBRES area. HOUTKERQUE — Supplies refilled on 6 Train wagons & delivered & units in new area for consumption 12th. Supplies for 14th dumped at RUBROUK — (No: 4 Co: at HOUTKERQUE). A Branch Engine Drives drove into a long mule Road during march of No: 2 Coy: with the result that 2 G.S. wagons were knocked over & smashed, 1 man killed & 2 injured — 2 horses killed. Full inquires made & Report submitted. THQ. & NIELLES. No: 2 Coy: to HENNEVEUX. No: 3 & SENLEQUES. No: 4. Co: COLUMBY.	
RUBROUK	13th	—		
NIELLES	16th	—	Nos: 2 & 4 Coys: exchange locations. Railhead LUMBRES.	
"	17th	—	Advance Parties of 28th American Division arrive. Supplied Meat & Tea & Biscuits at Detraining Point.	
"	19th	—	No: 2 Coy: draw & deliver Rations to American units	
"	20th	—	Hospital Companies. All in first rate order.	
"	21st	—	Hd Qrs American Division & other all units arrived	
"	24th	—	Visited Companies & Arr all Divis 15th attached to Americans — handed them & own rated Companies — hoff ballroom turned to become stack. Conditions — hoff ballroom turned to become stack

WAR DIARY or INTELLIGENCE SUMMARY

Army Form C. 2118

Place	Date	Hour	Summary of Events and Information	Remarks and references to Appendices
MELLES	26th May	—	9th N.F., 11th Suffolks, 1/1st Lancs: Leave Division Complete with Train Transport. 19.G.S. Wagons - Complete - handed over to American Troops. Capt. & Adj: E. Newell leave to "Q" for temporary duty. W. Smith assumed duties of Adjutant.	
"	31st	—	A.W. Alexander Lt. Col. O.C. Syl. Dist. Train.	

Secret   SA/152

H.Q.
6th Division G.

I beg to forward herewith
War Diary volume No 30 covering
period 1st 30th June 1918.

A W Alexander
Lieut Colonel
G.S. 6th Division

9-7-1918

Army Form C. 2118.

WAR DIARY
or
INTELLIGENCE SUMMARY.
(Erase heading not required.)

34 D Train Vol 30

Place	Date	Hour	Summary of Events and Information	Remarks and references to Appendices
NIELLES	June 1918			
"	1st		D.D.S. & T. II'd Army visited the Train & inspected No: 3 Coy: very good turn-out.	
"	2nd		S.S.O: proceeded on leave - Capt: WILLS-FLEMING took over his duties.	
"	3rd		No: 3 Coy: moved to HARDINGHEM - No. 4 to CONTEVILLE.	
"	4th		Train H.d.Q.rs moved to WIERRE EFFROI - Supplies for 102nd Bde drawn by No. 2 from LUMBRES - Remainder from SAMER.	
WIERREEFFROI	10th		Lt. Smith having proceeded on leave. 2/Lt GROVE took over duties of S.S.O.	
"	11		No: 2 Coy: moved to COLUMBY - No: 3 to HENNEVEUX - No: 4 to BRUNENBERT T.H.Q.	
	12th		KNELLES. Nos: 3 & 4 Coy; 4th Train formed for temporary duty	
NIELLES			Det. No. 4 Coy (under 2/Lt. TREW-) moved to BLEQUIN to supply American Units	
"	14th		in SENLEQUES Area.	
			Capt. & Adj. MEBRET - returns to duty . 3 Batt. MT. hire Transports arrived & were attached to No. 2 Co:	
"	15th		Lieut: A.R. LESLIE - "Mentioned in despatches"	
"	16th		S.S.O. returned from leave - 3 Divr Line Transports with No: 2 Coy: join 39th Division	
"	17th		Surplus Transport (in charge of Mr. BASKETT) to ABBEVILLE - Train H.O.Q. moved to MOULINET No: 2 Coy: to Bal Camp SAMER	

WAR DIARY
or
INTELLIGENCE SUMMARY

Army Form C. 2118

Place	Date	Hour	Summary of Events and Information	Remarks and references to Appendices
MOULINET	1918		Railhead DEVRES.	
"	19/2		No: 4 Coy: moved to HQDICR - 20 G.S. wagons 40 horses arrived from A.H.T. Depôt.	
"	20/6		No: 3 Coy: moved to S.C.C.6.3 (CALAIS) - Sergt: O'Gorman awarded Meritorious Service Medal.	
"	21/2		S.Sergt: Varner awarded Meritorious Service Medal	
"	22/2		2/Lt: Gunn to A.H.T. Depôt to take over Transport for 80th American Divn.	
"	23/2		2/Lt: Burkett - " - " - " - " -	
"	24/2		Transport arriving previous day handed over to Americans. Remainder of Transport handed over to Americans - Receipts taken. 2/Lt: Robson to A.H.T. Depôt to take over Transport for Americans.	
"	25/2		2/Lt: Snow - " - " - " - " -	
"	26/2		4.5 H.D. horses landed way to the Cherbourg Rails. Lieut: Hutton to A.H.T. Depôt to take over Transport for Americans. Riding Horses for Americans arrived from S.A.A. Depôt.	
"	27/2		Lieut: Smith to A.H.T. Depôt to collect Cookers for Americans. Repairing Truck.	
"	28/2		3 & 4 Train H.B.6/2 moved to ELVES. No: 2 Coy: to ELVES.	

WAR DIARY
or
INTELLIGENCE SUMMARY

(Erase heading not required.)

Army Form C. 2118

Place	Date	Hour	Summary of Events and Information	Remarks and references to Appendices
ELNES	29/2		THQ. to ST MOMELIN - also 3 Coys. Supplies drawn by M.T. from ROUSBRUGGE	
MOMELIN	30/2		THQ. G BAMBECQUES. No. 2 Coy. to MERZEELE - No. 3 & ROUSBRUGGE - No. 14 to ST JAN TER BIEZEN.	

AusT Alexander Lt. Col.
f.c. 34th Div. Train

SECRET

H.Q.
3rd Division G.S.

    I beg to forward herewith War Diary Volume No 31 Covering the period 1st to 31st July 1918. The delay in rendering same is regretted, owing to constant moves it was overlooked.

A.W. Alexander
Lieut Colonel
O/c 3rd District Train.

25-8-18

Army Form C. 2118.

34 D Train Original

WAR DIARY
or
INTELLIGENCE SUMMARY.
(Erase heading not required.)

Place	Date	Hour	Summary of Events and Information	Remarks and references to Appendices
BAMBEQUE	1st July 1918		Visited COUTHOVE CHATEAU - hus. Tram No. 9 X	
"	3rd		Move to COUTHOVE - No: 2 Coy to F.13 d. Cerkach Sheet 27.	
COUTHOVE	4th		Railhead ROUSBRUGGE.	
"	5th		No: 1 Coy Required - E. 10. d. 7.7.	
"	7th		MM: 1. 2. 3 Coys drew from Railway by H.T. No: 4 by M.T. to area at	
			Bouchen. No: 3 Coy. moved to ST JAN TER BIEZEN. No: 4 to ST OMER	
"	13th		No: 3 Coy to CORMETTE Area (ST OMER) No: 2 G ST JANNTER BIEZEN. No: 4 Pm	
			ST OMER to F. 13 d. Central.	
"	16th		No: 1 Coy, to SURVILLERS - to entrain	
"	17th		T.M.Q. entrain at WAANBEKE	
"	18th		T.M.Q. detrain at CHANTILLY - march to SENLIS	
"	19th		T.M.Q. to LARGNY - M: 1 - Bois DE TILLET. No: 4. VAUCIENNES. No: 3. VEZ. No: 2	
			L. Bois DE TILLET.	
"	20th		Railhead CHANTILLY. No: 1 Coy to LONGANEINE. No: 2 + 3. PUSIEUX. 4. SOMAY.	
"	21st		Railhead CREPY. THR to VIVIERES, all Companies	
"	22nd		Railhead VILLERS COTTERETS. THR. to Ground near LONGPONT.	

Army Form C. 2118

WAR DIARY
or
INTELLIGENCE SUMMARY
(Erase heading not required.)

Original

Place	Date	Hour	Summary of Events and Information	Remarks and references to Appendices
FOREST nr LONGPONT	27th -		Second Refilling in anticipation of move.	
"	29th		T.HQ. to CHOUY. No: 1 Coy to ROZET. Remaining Companies to NADON FARM. Supplies delivered by M.T. to new areas	

A.W. Alexander Lt:Col:
O.C: 34th Divisional Train.

34DT/125

H.Q
34th Division C.S.

I beg to forward herewith
War Diary volume No 32.
Covering period 1st to 31st August.
Delay regretted.

16/9/18.

[signature]
Capt & Adjt
for Lieut Colonel
Comdg. 34 Div Train

Army Form C. 2118.

34 D Train
Vol 3 ²

WAR DIARY
or
INTELLIGENCE SUMMARY.
(Erase heading not required.)

Instructions regarding War Diaries and Intelligence Summaries are contained in F. S. Regs., Part II. and the Staff Manual respectively. Title pages will be prepared in manuscript.

Place	Date	Hour	Summary of Events and Information	Remarks and references to Appendices
CHOUY	1st August 1918.		The K.D. Remounts arrived at Railhead.	
"	2nd		Remounts handed over to Reserve Brigade Admin.	
"	3rd		Supplies dumped in New Area W. of GERAMENIL FARM.	
			Train H.Qrs. moved to BILLY. No.1 Coy. to ROZET. No. 2, 3, 4th to same area.	
BILLY	4th		Supplies drawn from CREPY & dumped near entraining stations. 2, 3, 4 Coys. entrain under Brigade Arrangements. No.1. marched under orders of C.R.A.	
			Train H.Qrs. to NAREUIL.	
NAREUIL	5th		Train H.Qrs. to NANTEUIL. Supplies for Cavalry Corps. 7th Hrd Rations for Train.	
			Journey for 6th carried in supply trapin.	
NANTEUIL	6th		Train H.Qrs. entrained at NANTEUIL.	
ESQUELBECQ	7th		Train H.Qrs. detrained at REXPOEDE & marched to ESQUELBECQ No: 1 Co. K. 9.4.9. Sheet 27. No. 2 at ESQUELBECQ. No. 3 at BERGUES - ZEGGERS CAPEL Road No: 4 at WORMHOUT.	
			Railhead ROUSBRUGGE - M.T. draw - Train Transport Refills.	
"	8th		Officers & O.R. received decorations from the French, the following -	
			Lieut Col. A.W. Alexander Croix-de-Guerre. (1st Class)	
			Major Rd. Sketheare D.S.O.)	
			Capt. & Adj. S.K. Menret) (2nd Class)	
			Lieut Jn. Ritson) Croix de Guerre
			Sergt Barclay) (2nd Class)
			Cpl. A. Morine
			Cpl. Hancock

WAR DIARY or INTELLIGENCE SUMMARY

Army Form C. 2118.

Place	Date	Hour	Summary of Events and Information	Remarks and references to Appendices
ESQUELBECQ	August 11th		107th Bde Supplied twice. Off. Train + 10 NCOs + men to TERDINGHEM for special Church Parade. H.M. The King present	
"	12th		No: 1 Coy. draw from Railhead by H.T. No: 1 Coy moved to HANDEKOT. No: 2 to ST MARTIN AU LAERT (Training Area). Nos: 3 & 4 Coys supplied twice	
"	13th		No: 4 Coy. to ST JAN TER BIEZEN. No: 3 to HERZEELE	
"	14th		No: 3 Coy. draws from Railhead by H.T.	
"	16th		No: 4 Coy. to E.12. F.1.8. Sheet 27.	
"	18th		Railhead INTERNATIONAL CORNER. Supplies drawn by M.T. No: 4 Coy	
"	19th		to BARNES FARM	
"	20th		No: 4 Coy. draws from Railhead by H.T.	
"	21st		Nos: 1 & 3 Coys. draw supplies by H.T.	
"			No: 3 Coy. to A. 3.d. 4.3. Sheet 28. Train HDqrs to LA LOVIE CHATEAU	
LA LOVIE	22nd		No: 2 Coy to K ZEGGERS CAPEL. No: 1 Coy. to F.16. a. 3.4.	
"	23rd		No: 2 Coy to E.12.d.3.8. Supplies for all Brigades drawn by M.T.	
"	24th		Supplies drawn by M.T. in view of projection by Corps Commander. (Cancelled.)	
"	26th		Supplies drawn by M.T. Lt. Col. Alexander to PARIS on 5 days leave. Major R.A. Shepheard D.S.O. (late) ODC Command of Train. Capt. Plunkett S.S.O.	

2353. Wt. W25H/1454 700,000 5/15 D.D.&L. A.D.S.S./Forms/C. 2118.

WAR DIARY
or
INTELLIGENCE SUMMARY
(Erase heading not required.)

Army Form C. 2118.

Place	Date	Hour	Summary of Events and Information	Remarks and references to Appendices
LA LOVIE	27th (continued)		No: 3 Coy to ROAD CAMP - Supplies drawn by M.T.	
"	28th		No: 2 Coy to R.26.d.7.9. Pheer 27. No.3.b - COIMETTE Area.	
"	29th		Train HQ & K.21, K.9 & Sheet 27 -	
			attached to 16th Divl: Train. No 1 Coy 44th Train attached to 34th	
			Divl: Train Supplies for 101st 102nd & 13th Other drawn by M.T.	
			delivered to new area. 103rd. B46. refill area.	
R.21.b.9.4	30th		Supply Railhead for 101st 102nd & 13th ESQUELBECQ Drawn by M.T.	
"	31st		" " 103rd B46 - STEENVOORDE Lt. Col. Alexander	
			having returned from leave, resumed command of the Train.	

A.W. Alexander Lt=Col:
M. 34th Divl. Train.

6   Hot 151.

S.B.
  4th Division G.S.

        Herewith please find
War Diary volume 33 for period
1st to 31st September.
  Delay regretted

                    [signature]
                    Lieut Colonel
25/10/18   Cmdg Div Train A.S.C.

Army Form C. 2118.

WAR DIARY
or
INTELLIGENCE SUMMARY.
(Erase heading not required.)

34 D Train Vol 33

Instructions regarding War Diaries and Intelligence Summaries are contained in F. S. Regs., Part II. and the Staff Manual respectively. Title pages will be prepared in manuscript.

Place	Date	Hour	Summary of Events and Information	Remarks and references to Appendices
	September 1918			
K.21.b.4.4.	1st Sept		Train H.Qrs moved to L.28.b.3.4. Sheet 27. No.4 Coy. K.L.32.a.2.9. No.2. & R.27.a.7.5.	
	2nd		Refilling by 1st Aux Transport at ABEELE Aerodrome. Supplies drawn by M.T. conveyed to new Refilling Point. Sheet 28. G.32.d.9.4. B.H.Q. Group remain at Aerodrome.	
L.28. G.3.4.	2nd		No. 1 Coy: 6 K.17.B.8.5. No. 2 L.32.d.7.4. No.3: L.29.C.8.2. No.4 L.34.C.3.5.	
"	5th		No. 1 Coy. G 27/L.7.C.2.8.	
"	7th		Railhead WIPPENHOEK	
"	9th		103rd Bde refilled Road. No. 4 Coy: G 27/K.27.C.3.1. Major Tweedy struck off strength	
"	10th		hand. A.D. Smith appointed D.A.D Crown Offices.	
"	11th		Supplies drawn for 103rd Bde by M.T.	
"	12th		No. 4 Coy: WESTNOENT.	
"	13th		No. 3 Coy: Camp Shelled - Coy. moved to 27/L.34 C.3.6.	
"	17th		103rd Bde drawn from VIIIth Corps Parcels at WATTEN	
27/R.S.C.7	18th		Train H.Qrs. G 27/R.S.C.7. No. 3 K. 27/R.S.C.7.6.	
"	20th		102nd Bde refilled Train convoy to Camps. Roll 1033 Bde were cancelled	
"	21st		No.4 Coy: G 27/R.S.D.2.5. Train Training Area.	
"	23rd		Supplies for 102 & 103 drawn by M.T. from WATTEN. Oil supply from WIPPENHOEK.	

Army Form C. 2118.

WAR DIARY
or
INTELLIGENCE SUMMARY.
(Erase heading not required.)

Place	Date	Hour	Summary of Events and Information	Remarks and references to Appendices
27/R.S.C.17	26ᵈ Sept.		Refilled Trains. A.O.C. Division inspected all Companies & expressed satisfaction.	
"	27ᵗʰ		A.D.S.T. IIⁿᵈ Army inspected No: 1 & 3 Coys:	
"	29ᵗʰ		No: 1 Coy: 6 & 24/h. 31- 1.8.2. No: 2 v 3 1: - 28/M.6.a.9.9. No: 4 15 20/M.6.a.8.4	
"	30ᵗʰ		Very battered Camp - practically no shelter. Railhead OUDERDOM	

A.S. Alexander Lt.Col.
O.C. 34ᵗʰ Divisional Train.

By Registered Post.　　　　　　　　　S-E C R E T.

D.A.G,　　　　　　　　　　　　　　　　　G.M. 1/24.
3rd Echelon.

   Herewith War Diary of 34th Divisional Train for the month of October, 1918.

   The delay in completing this diary is regretted.

                 C. Levy
                Brigadier General,
27th December, 1918.　　　　　　Commanding 34th Division.

34

34 D Train Army Form C. 2118.

WAR DIARY
or
INTELLIGENCE SUMMARY.
(Erase heading not required.)

Place	Date	Hour	Summary of Events and Information	Remarks and references to Appendices
28. M.6.	1/10/18		Train Coy. were under orders of C.R.A. and Brigades respectively from M.6. & advanced area HOUTHEM-HOLLEBEKE. All Coys. reported escape casualties from enemy shelling.	
HOUTHEM- HOLLEBEKE	2		Accordingly selected camps further back. No reply today. Railhead RENINGHELST drawn by Train Tpt. Drawing by M.T. from Railhead OUDERDOM. R.P. f Brigades Tpt. at KONIGSTRAATHOEK in KEMMEL Rd.	
	3		Train Coy. were under orders of C.R.A. & Brigades to new selected camps.	do
			Ground almost impossible for Transport Coy. moving to Hell Blas. which has some extent	do
			shelter in Dressing room nor as a 2nd refilly by Train transport.	
28.H.36.	5		T.H.Q. & C.R.A.'s H.Q. of convenience have remained at L.27/R.5.a near new D.H.Q. moved to KRUIG- STRAATHOEK.	
28.H.20.d	6		Lt. Col. R.J. ALEXANDER on leave to U.K. 7/10/18 - 21/10/18	
	7		Major R.A. SHEBBEAR D.S.O. takes over temporary command of Train T/Lieut. C.E. DUNKIN takes over duties of S.S.O. 2 Train drivers 1 Farrier M.G.C. and 3 horses killed	
			by shell fire at ZANDVOORDE. 7/10. HALLER shewed great coolness rabbit hutch	
			enemy shelling.	
	8		In view of intense shelling & state of roads an advanced park annual R.P. 62c was established at HOLLEBEKE. New Train wagons delivered instead of Wagon Lines.	

Army Form C. 2118.

WAR DIARY
or
INTELLIGENCE SUMMARY.
(Erase heading not required.)

Instructions regarding War Diaries and Intelligence Summaries are contained in F. S. Regs., Part II. and the Staff Manual respectively. Title pages will be prepared in manuscript.

Place	Date	Hour	Summary of Events and Information	Remarks and references to Appendices
28/H 30.d	9		Moved from routine as shown in foregoing slips. Advanced pits R.P. increased	
"	17		T.H.Q. L- J.32.c. Central 28.f. No.3. 2 v 4 Coys: Ditto. 1 Coy: L- R.27.a Central. No.3.	
			L J.32. c.1.8.	
J.32.C.	18		T.H.Q. L 28.f. Q.4.c.7.6. GHELUVE	
GHELUVE	19		T.H.Q. L 28/8.6.6.3½. M/Coy: L Q.4.c.3½. No. 2 v 3.6. Q.0.a.3.7. No.4.6.0.6.a.2.2.	
			Refilling points GHELUVE-WERWICQ Road	
28/Q.4.6.3.6.	20		Reached DEKENEBEK	
"	21		Refilling by Train Transport – T.H.Q. L- 28/ R.14.c.2.6. M/Coy. L 28/R.23.d.3.6.	
20/R.14.c.2.6.			No. 2 L 28/R.6.a.8.7. No. 3.L-28/R.16.a.3.7. No. 4 L 28/R.15.c.6.6.	
"	22.		T.H.Q. L LAUWE – No. 2 Coy: L 28/R.17.a. No.3.L. 20/R.29.6.1.7. No. 4 L 25/R.8.c.a.6.	
LAUWE	23		Lt. Col. ALEXANDER returns from leave.	
"	26.		Battle Reg.d for Div. Troops 102 v 103 2nd Bde. No. 2 Coy: MUISTE	
"	27		M.4 Coy. L- 29/L.4.c.3.7.	
"	28		No. 3 Coy. L 29/B.2.3.d.4.7. No.4 L- 29/B.6.c.	
"	29		T.H.Q. L 29/H.11.6.2.9. No. 3 Coy. L 4/H.4. No.2 L 1.7.6.9a.	
29/H.11.6.2.9	30		No. 2 Coy. L B.18.c.9.5. M.2 Coy. Group trained. 1 man wounded. 9 horses wounded.	2/Lt Alexander K./H.M. L/S 34 R. Nfld. Fran.

(A9175) Wt W3358/P156 600,000 12/17 D. D. & L. Sch. 52a- Forms/C2118/15

"Original"
34 D Train
Army Form C. 2118.

WAR DIARY
or
INTELLIGENCE SUMMARY.
(Erase heading not required.)

Place	Date	Hour	Summary of Events and Information	Remarks and references to Appendices
29/H.11.b.2.9.	November 1918.			
"	3rd	-	T.H.Q. moved to 28/4. 23.a.9.4. No:1 Coy. to 29/G.32.d.7.5. No:2 to 29/M.2.d.4.3.	
"			No:3 to 28/4.17.a.1.7.- No:4 to 29/G.28.d.0.4.	
28/4. 23.a.9.4.	6th	-	Supplies drawn from HEULE by Horse Transport. Refilling by 10th Line	
"	7th	-	No:1 Coy. to 29/T.16. Supplies for Div. Troops drawn by M.T.	
"	8th	-	No:4 Coy. to R.20.c. Central. Supplies for 103rd Bde. also drawn by M.T.	
"	11th	-	No:1 Coy. to 29/O.S.6.6.3. 2 Officers Chargers stolen by unkn-horse No:2 Coy	
"	12th	-	No:1 Coy. to 29/A.32.A.7.5.	
"	14th	-	No:2 Coy. to SIGENON - No:3 to ROLEGHEM - No:4 to MALCENCE Area. Supplies	
"			drawn by M.T. Refilling by Train Transport.	
"	15th	-	T.H.Q. to WATTRIPONT. No:1 Coy. to ORCHEM. Area. No:2 to ANSEROEUL Area.	
			No.3. to CELLES Area. No:4. to MOUSCRON 412 Area. 50 men from Div. Supply col.	
			Coy arrived & attes loading. Major STEBBETRE on leave. Capt. WILLIS -	
			Relieved takes over duties of I.S.O.	
WATTRIPONT	16th	-	No:1 Coy. to ANVAING Area. No:2 to ELLIZELLE Area. No.3 to CINQUANT	
			Area. No:4 to 27/0. a.a.3.3. 20 G.S. Waggons from No.7 Army	
			Auxilliary H.T. Coy. Recevd - in more.	

Army Form C. 2118.

WAR DIARY
or
INTELLIGENCE SUMMARY.
(Erase heading not required.)

Instructions regarding War Diaries and Intelligence Summaries are contained in F. S. Regs., Part II, and the Staff Manual respectively. Title pages will be prepared in manuscript.

Place	Date	Hour	Summary of Events and Information	Remarks and references to Appendices
WATTRIPONT	18th	Nov=	THQ to LESSINES. No. 1 Coy. to 38/ A.H.d.F.9 - No.2 6- 2 Km. S. of LESSINES. No. 3 to FLOBECQ - No. 4 ORY-LESSINES Road - Railhead COURTRAI.	
LESSINES	21st		Wagons from A.H.T. Coy. to 29th Division. Railhead VICHTE.	
	23rd		RAILHEAD - HERSEAUX.	
	28th		Railhead - TOURNAI.	

A.S. Alexander Lt. Col.
O.C. 34th Div. Sup. Train.

Per Registered Post   G.M. 1/29.

D. A. G.,
    3rd ECHELON

        Herewith War Diary of 34th Divisional Train
for period 1st - 31st December, 1918.

                                    [signature]
                                        Major General,
2-2-19.   Commanding 34th Division.

WAR DIARY or INTELLIGENCE SUMMARY

Army Form C. 2118.

34th Divisional Train

Vol 36

Place	Date	Hour	Summary of Events and Information	Remarks and references to Appendices
LESSINES	December 1918			
"	5th		Railhead CHISLINGHEM.	
"	6th		Farm at OGY. Butter & No:1 Coy; almost immed. down. no damage to Personnel or animals, but some equipment destroyed. County opening heavy.	
"	11th		Several Refugees moving Eastwar	
"	12th		Railhead BRAINE-LE-COMTE. Train T.H.Q. to SOIGNIES No:1 Coy to 3's/ J.1-1-1-6-7. No:2 to SOIGNIES - No:3 to SILLY. No:4 to LOT	
SOIGNIES	14th		No:1 Coy to HOURDES. No:2 to HOUDENG. No:3 to LA QUELENDE - No:4 to SOIGNIES	
"	16th		T.H.Q. to COURCELLES - No:1 Coy to LA LOUVIERES - No:2 to ROUX - No:3 to HAINE ST PIERRE No:4 to CHAPELLE-LEZ-HERAIMONT.	
COURCELLES	17th		No:1 Coy to SOUVRET - No:2 to MONTIGNIES - No:4 to CHARLEROI	
"	18th		T.H.Q. to CHATELET. No:1 Coy to CHATELET - No:2 to SART-ST LAURENT. No:3 to BOUFFIOULX - No:4 to PRESLES.	
CHATELET	19th		Railhead TAMINES. T.H.Q. to PROFONDVILLE - No:1 Coy to BUGNOT. No:3 to NEUVREMONT - No:4 to FOOZ	

Army Form C. 2118.

WAR DIARY
or
INTELLIGENCE SUMMARY.
(Erase heading not required.)

Instructions regarding War Diaries and Intelligence Summaries are contained in F. S. Regs., Part II. and the Staff Manual respectively. Title pages will be prepared in manuscript.

Place	Date	Hour	Summary of Events and Information	Remarks and references to Appendices
PROFONDVILLE	30th		Railhead NAMUR	
"	23rd		No 4 Coy to AUVELAIS	
"	24th		Capt. Yates, MERRET on leave to U.K. Capt. SMITH taken over duties of Adjutant	
"	25th		Refilling by Train Transport	
"	26th		Railhead FLOREFFE	
"	27th		Refilling by 1st Line Transport. No 1 Coy to BUZET No 2 to SAUCE	
"			No 4 to SART ST LAURENT	
"	28th		Supplies drawn from Railhead by Train wagons.	

MS Alexander Lt.Col.
O.C. 34th Div. Train

Army Form C. 2118.

WAR DIARY
or
INTELLIGENCE SUMMARY.
(Erase heading not required.)

Place	Date	Hour	Summary of Events and Information	Remarks and references to Appendices
PROFONDEVILLE			JANUARY 1919	
PROFONDEVILLE	1/1/19		Railhead FLOREFFE	
"	7/1/19		3 Siamese officers attached for 7 days	
"	17/1/19		No.4 Co. move to TAMINES	
"	"		No.2 Co. entrain AWELAIS for GERMANY location BUISDORF	
"	20/1/19		No.4 " " TAMINES " NEIDER PLEIS	
"	22/1/19		No.3 " " AWELAIS " BEUEL	
"	"		No.1 " move to NEVRE MONT	
"	24/1/19		Train HQ entrain NAMUR for Germany location SEIGBURG	
SEIGBURG	25/1/19		No.1 Co. entrain AWELAIS for TROISDORF GERMANY	
"	27/1/19		Railhead SEIGBURG	
"	31/1/19		No.3 Co. move to TROISDORF	

90 Boyle Coff
Lt Col Commanding
OC 34 Train

Army Form C. 2118.

WAR DIARY
or
INTELLIGENCE SUMMARY.
(Erase heading not required.)

Vol 36

Place	Date	Hour	Summary of Events and Information	Remarks and references to Appendices
SEIGBURG	FEBRUARY 1919			
SEIGBURG	2nd		No 4 Co. moved to SEIGBURG	
	9th		T/CAPT. A.D. SMITH appointed adjutant vice T/CAPT. E.L. MERRETT (with effect from 9.1.19) (unestablished) Auth X Corps No A 9/29/72	
	11th		G.O.C. inspected Cos. of the Train	
	12th		T/MAJOR R.A. SHEBBEARE found unfit by Medical Board & struck off strength from 17/1/19 Auth. QMG GHQ No R.P./ASC 2227 8/30/1/19	
	14th		CAPT. A.E.H. LEE struck off strength from 6/2/19 Auth. QMG No R.P./ASC 222 30/2 & 6/2/19	
	23rd		No 2 Co. moved to SEIGBURG No 4 Co. to BUISDORF	
	25th		CAPT. A.E.A. SHORT joined for duty from 21st Div Train vice CAPT A.E.H. LEE	
	26th		T/2nd LIEUT R.L.M. CRUICKSHANK struck off strength & proceeded to Concentration Camp for demobilization	
	26th		T/LIEUT E.P. RIVAZ " "	
	27th		T/2nd LIEUT A.C. CRISP taken over duties of Claims Officer from 2nd LIEUT A.L. BARTON with effect from 27/2/19	

J.J. Boyd Capt
for Lt Col
OC 8th Train

L. Dunsmuir
OC 8th

Army Form C. 2118.

WAR DIARY
or
INTELLIGENCE SUMMARY.
(Erase heading not required.)

WO 39

Place	Date	Hour	Summary of Events and Information	Remarks and references to Appendices
SIEGBURG	1st March 1919		Capt. WILLIS-FLEMING to No.1 Coy, while acting as S.S.O.	
"	4th		2/Lieut. FREW appointed S.O. 103rd Bde.	
"	5th		Capt. BUTLE assumed Command of the Train on departure of Lt. Col. ALEXANDER on leave	
"	9th		Lieut. BARTON demobilised	
"	11th		22 Horses Class Z. to Animal Collecting Camp - COLOGNE, in exchange for equivalent number of X Horses	
"	15th		34th Division re-named "EASTERN" Division	
"	16th		13 "X" Horses Collected from COLOGNE. Three one of Nulljahgast Quielle	
"	19th		40 "Z" Horses despatched.	
"	24th		Lieut. Col. ALEXANDER returned from leave resumed Command of the Train	
"	25th		Lieut. BURTON joined the Train. 2/Lieut. CRUICKSHANK demobilised	
"	26th		Major WILLIAMS joined the Train - posted to No.1 Coy.	
"	29th		Major BLACKBURN joined the Train. Appointed S.S.O.	

OS Alexander Lt.Col.
OC Eastern Div. Train

T/134

Instructions regarding War Diaries and Intelligence Summaries are contained in F. S. Regs., Part II, and the Staff Manual respectively. Title pages will be prepared in manuscript.

WAR DIARY
or
INTELLIGENCE SUMMARY.
(Erase heading not required.)

Army Form C. 2118.

Place	Date	Hour	Summary of Events and Information	Remarks and references to Appendices
SIEGBURG - MAY - 1919				
	1		T/Lieut A.K. Leslie resumes duties of S.O. 1st Inf Bde.	
	3		6 O. Ranks enter concentration Camp for Demobilization	
	8		Informed by A.D.S. Rhine Army that all R.E. personnel in Division are to be demobilized shortly, therefore applied to Division for 150 Infantry personnel to be sent to replace & for a further 100 in a weeks time.	
	10		T/Lieut F.G. Curtain takes up War Office appointment & is struck off strength.	
			20 O.Rs enter Concentration Camp for demobilization	
	12		T/Lieut R.B. Grove proceeded to 12th Div Sigs & is struck off strength.	
	13		T/Lieut F. Atkins assumes duties of S.O. 3rd Inf Bde.	
	14		T/Lieut A.H. Coxt? resumes duties of 2nd post subaltern with No 1 Co.	
			T/Capt H.L. Westbrook resumes duties of O.C. No 2 Company.	
	16		14 O.Rs enter Concentration Camp for demobilization	
	17		100 Infantry personnel attached	
	19		T/Capt H.L. Westbrook takes over duties of S.O. 1st Inf Bde.	
			T/Lieut A.K. Leslie takes over duties of S.O. Div Troops.	

(A9175) Wt W2358/P360 600,000 12/7 D. D. & L. Sch. 52a. Forms/C2118/15

WAR DIARY
or
INTELLIGENCE SUMMARY.
(Erase heading not required.)

Army Form C. 2118.

Place	Date	Hour	Summary of Events and Information	Remarks and references to Appendices
	19		Lieut Col. Alexander took over duties of O.C. & Hon. Officer	
	21		O.R.V.S. & baggage arrived. Arrival of Horses & Drivers.	
			Lieut Q.C. Boys entered Inspection Camp for Inoculation ceasing again off	
	22		2nd Lieut Trevelyn joined from R.F.C. Camp at Rouen 10 shifts to be shop	
	23		2nd Lieut entered Inoculation Camp for Inoculation	
	24		2 Subalterns R.A.S.C. transferred from Rouen Company Ord. & Repair Co.	
			Lieut Col Trevenen & Lt.Col. but remaining attached for duty undoubtedly ill	
			Lieut August.	
	27		½ and ½ Lieut J. Trevelyn to MARTENTZURG with supplies Command	

Sgd Alexander Lt Col
Comdg
Longe Reclam No Comp

WAR DIARY or INTELLIGENCE SUMMARY

Army Form C. 2118.

(Erase heading not required.)

Place	Date	Hour	Summary of Events and Information	Remarks and references to Appendices
SEIGBURG	JUNE 1919.			
	1st		Battalion taken over from Seaforth Highlanders by H.T. Robertson by Capt. Marshall	
	3		Guard came over from 1st Army Rest (Repr) Co. & posted to No. 1 C.	
	7		New Officers' Concentration Camp for Sub-officers	
	8		1 Lieut U.S. Prisoner arrived from Northern Diff prison & posted to No. 2 C. & returned Dublin	
			Capt S.O. 1st Batt. S.W.B.	
	9		Lieut (TF) W. Charm reported to depot	
			Major R.E.J. Blaylack proceeded on leave to U.K. for time 9/9 to 9/9	
			Captain & Adjt. M. Lowe hands 1 M.C. assumed duties as S.S.A. during absence of Major R.E.J. Blaylack	
			2 Lieut F.N. Mills M.C. assumed duties as Acting Adjutant	
	12		Lieut A.N. Mills 2nd Batt M.C. & Lieut Llewellyn gazette Lieut's to war dept of	
			Irregiment pending gazette.	
			S.O. Co. entered concentration camp for demobilization	
	14		Shelling of billets on arrival at Suresnes arrived in case of prearranged	
	18		hostilities	
	19		Last announcement to concentration area No. 6 to HENNEF No. 26 to HENNEF	

WAR DIARY or INTELLIGENCE SUMMARY

Army Form C. 2118.

Place	Date	Hour	Summary of Events and Information	Remarks and references to Appendices
(continued)	19		No 3 Co. moved billet at BULLDORF - bivouac. Pt Co. to Ing E.R.	
			Supplies drawn from Ind. billet by M.T.	
	20		Pont 1 (Willich) over from 3g Cav Bde. Pt Co. speck to 1 2 Co.	
	21		Pont. Rd. Wellich strengthened, found camph or bridging for emergency replacing.	
			Reserve of 3 ponds. Vehicle pts strength from ind. at Ind. Co. Rd. Pt. ITISBURG (Bucg.) 11/10½	
			No Co. reconnaissance routes for depot.	
	26		Pont Willich arrived from BDE to NT Co. speck to 1 2 Co.	
	28		L.O.R. concentration routes for demobilisation.	
			Reconnaissance pond.	
	30		No 1 Co. returned to former billet at TROISDORF. No 2 Co. moved to BULLDORF.	
			No 3 Co. moved to TROISDORF.	

Ans Alexander
Lieut Col
Comdg. 11th Lewd Div Engineers

Army Form C. 2118.

WAR DIARY
or
INTELLIGENCE SUMMARY.
(Erase heading not required.)

Place	Date	Hour	Summary of Events and Information	Remarks and references to Appendices
SIEGBURG	July 1919			
	1		[illegible handwritten entries]	
	2			
	6			
	13			
	14			
	16			
	17			
	19			
	21			
	30			
	31			

www.ingramcontent.com/pod-product-compliance
Lightning Source LLC
Chambersburg PA
CBHW081539160426
43191CB00011B/1791